PROLETARIANS AND PARTIES

Five essays in social class

Leslie Benson

TAVISTOCK PUBLICATIONS

First published in 1978 by
Methuen Publications (N.Z.) Ltd,
238 Wakefield Street, Wellington, N.Z.

Published in Great Britain in 1978 by
Tavistock Publications Ltd,
11 New Fetter Lane, London EC4.

ISBN 0 422 76580 5

Printed in Hong Kong

BA

BA CO

Proletarians and Parties

Contents

Errata

Contents: Chapter 4 - for Words read Worlds

Page 98, line 18: the following material should run on.

for Hilda and John

Preface

This book has been written with a particular public in mind. In this university I have become increasingly involved in the teaching of extramural students, whose opportunities for personal contact with either their teachers or their fellow students are frequently extremely limited. At the same time, extramural students take courses which in all essential respects must conform to those of their full-time counterparts. In this book, therefore, I have tried to construct a sort of do-it-yourself kit on which to base a year-long introductory course concerned with social class. It can be read in two somewhat different, though obviously closely related, ways. Each chapter, considered singly, deals with a theme, the main issues and concepts of which are raised and discussed, where possible in relation to empirical work. On this level, the five chapters comprise as many study guides, each complete in itself. From another (at least as important) point of view, they read cumulatively, as an attempt to provide students with a grounding in the historical and comparative analysis of variations in capitalist class structures. Despite the very great difficulties in the way of achieving much depth in a book of this kind, it still seems to me essential not to lose sight altogether of this second aim. I have tried not to do so, although I now realise much better than I did that the enterprise produces many more questions than answers.

A number of my colleagues have taken a friendly interest in the book and have helped by reading parts of it, for which I am grateful to them. Zora, James and David have helped in other ways, especially by being so patient during the writing of it.

Leslie Benson

Massey University
November 1977

1 Conflict and progress: 'class' in the work of Marx

Marx* was not a theorist of social stratification, at least in the sense that the phrase is nowadays frequently interpreted and applied to the study of social inequalities. That is to say, he was not interested in examining a given order of inequality at a fixed point in time, although certainly his intellectual energy was fuelled by a sharp intolerance of injustice and by his humane vision of a classless society. His preoccupation with classes derived from his belief that he could explain why classes form and come into conflict with one another; and why their struggles resulted in the revolutionary overthrow of the hitherto ruling class. In other words, Marx undertook the analysis of those fundamental social processes which provoke the change from one distinctive form of social organisation (*epoch*, he called it) to another, and which show themselves historically in the form of class struggles and their attendant political and social revolutions.

The reasoning behind Marx's model of social change can be represented in two logical steps. Firstly, he saw the economic organisation of a given type of society as tending to undergo a process of change, because men continually enlarge their mastery over nature through technological innovation. Imperceptible in the early phases of the natural history

* You should understand that we are also talking about the work of Engels, to some extent. However, it is convenient to refer to Marx alone, and this is the usual practice.

of an epoch, the pressure towards such innovation builds up as it becomes clear that the existing economic organisation of society (in his phrase 'the productive forces') is faltering in its capacity to create the wealth necessary for the needs of its people. The sign of such a change is a shift in emphasis from one resource (slaves, land and capital) as the dominant means of production upon which ancient society, feudal society and bourgeois society were respectively founded.

The link between a given means of production and its corresponding societal type is established by Marx through the second step in his chain of argument. The different means of production, he reasoned, entail differing structures of social organisation designed to co-ordinate and control the human labour which alone can utilise resources to create wealth. Indeed, the means of production only *become* means of production through human activity, so that the term necessarily implies an appropriate set of *social relations of production*, by which the functioning of the economic system is sustained. What is more, in Marx's view the other institutions in society — legal, political, educational and so on — have as their central purpose the fostering and protection of the dominant relations of production. This phrase, in fact, which might otherwise be taken to refer to only the social relations governing activity in production, becomes a synonym for society itself, and Marx also tends to use the term *mode of production* with a similar meaning.

Of course, to say that societal institutions are interdependent is a sociological platitude. Marx gives this perception a peculiar twist, and turns it into a powerful analytical weapon, by asserting that the history of human societies is intelligible in terms of changes in organisation for production:

> 'In production, men not only act on nature but also on one another. They produce only by co-operating in a certain way and mutually exchanging their activities. In order to produce, they enter into definite connections and relations with one another, and only within these social connections and relations does their action on nature, does production, take place. . . .

Thus the social relations within which individuals produce, the social relations of production, change, are transformed, with the change and development of the material means of production, the productive forces. The relations of production in their totality constitute what are called the social relations, society, and, specifically, a society at a definite stage of historical development, a society with a peculiar, distinctive character. Ancient society, feudal society, bourgeois society are such totalities of production relations, each of which at the same time denotes a special stage of development in the history of mankind' (MESW: 81).

This formulation of the basic premises of the materialist conception of history appears in *Wage Labour and Capital*, a lecture to a nineteenth century working-class audience. The philosophical basis of historical materialism is developed more fully, but still with useful brevity, in the early parts of *The German Ideology*. Man (the argument runs) exists in nature only as a social being. That is, co-operation and exchange between individuals is the precondition of the development of the human faculties, which is itself a product of the environment. Men's original relationship to nature is entirely passive. They depend for their subsistence upon what nature provides, for example in hunting and gathering communities. This involves social organisation and co-operation, but not *action upon nature*, which to Marx is the specifically human attribute:

> 'Men can be distinguished from animals by consciousness, by religion or anything else you like. They themselves begin to distinguish themselves from animals as soon as they begin to *produce* their means of subsistence, a step which is conditioned by their physical organisation' (MECW: 31).

At a critical moment in the remote past, that is, their relationship to nature became an active one. Men make tools and develop a rudimentary technology. They display the planning and forethought necessary to sustain pastoral and agricultural activity. Each different type of economy constrains the physical and social organisation of its peoples, hence their mode of life and social existence. Men constantly improve their economic arrangements to satisfy their needs, however, and the natural history of society is one of increasing differentiation and specialisation of function as a direct result; each stage is marked by a more complex division of labour. Each stage, too, has its own forms of property — 'property', that is, defined as the rules and customs which stipulate who has the right to dispose of social wealth. In its earliest form — tribal property — there is little division of labour, little surplus wealth produced which can be appropriated, and therefore relative equality within a communal unit of production and consumption. Each step in the intensification of the division of labour has taken society further away from any communality of condition. The scale and productiveness of economic organisation creates the basis for the emergence of a class of non-producers, i.e., of people whose activity depends on the value-generating labour of others. Thus Marx makes the existence of the state, of classes, and of private property in the means of production hang upon the development of the division of labour. In this sense, men's material life, their action upon nature through co-operative labour to reproduce their wants, determines the forms of the state, property and classes which different societies exhibit. The economic order is the core institutional focus of change, and no matter how elaborate and diversified the 'superstructure' may be, it is still made up (according to Marx) of secondary and derivative institutions. The term 'division of labour', in fact, refers not only to functional specialisation in production, but also to the distribution of power and authority in society at large. As Marx puts it in the context of his discussion of capitalism, 'To define bourgeois property means no less than to describe all the social conditions of bourgeois production' (see the discussion in Dahrendorf 1959:11-12). All ruling classes have in common that they organise and control the production process, appropriating surplus labour to maintain their domination. Associated with the propertied/propertyless dichotomy which Marx takes as the defining criterion of class membership, therefore, are the other logically exhaustive pairs of attributes which constantly crop up in his writings: exploiting/exploited, and politically dominant/subordinate.

Each new level of development of the productive forces transforms not only societal relations but also signals a new phase in the unfolding of human knowledge. 'Knowledge' in this context must be understood in its widest sense, and includes not only the natural and social sciences, but also the complex of beliefs, ideas and values through which men simultaneously interpret the world and direct their own activities within it. 'Consciousness' is not, for Marx, a universal and timeless category; it is, on the contrary, a socially conditioned phenomenon. At any point in time, human consciousness is the outcome of the interplay between man and nature; or better put, the forms of human consciousness and man's active relationship to nature (labour) change each other. Marx shows us what he means in his comments on the origins and development of language, that peculiarly human skill which is the expression and precondition of culture. Language and consciousness are co-extensive; 'language, like consciousness, only arises from the need, the necessity, of intercourse with other men' (MECW:44). Language reflects the flux in material conditions of existence, for new concepts and new categories of speech are invented to cope with changing circumstances: 'At a certain stage of development, after both men's needs and the activity through which they are satisfied, have been enlarged and augmented, they will baptise with their language this category with which they have become acquainted by their experience' (quoted by Avineri 1968:74).

Homo sapiens, in Marx's version of the evolutionary process, thus makes his appearance as *homo faber* – man the do-er, the activist, the problem-solver. These problems do not pose themselves as intellectual puzzles but are on the contrary the outcome of tasks faced during the course of practical, day-to-day activity. It follows, then, that Marx does not operate with a static conception of human nature. The manifest differences between the members of societies as unalike as (say) the United States and an Australian aboriginal tribe in our own day do not conceal underlying similarities traceable to a common humanity. In Marx's pithy aphorism, 'As individuals express themselves, so they are.' As man develops his productive forces through labour, he develops what is essentially human in himself, the power to conceptualise, to draw on knowledge in order to change nature, and so change his own nature and knowledge, in a never-ending cycle. Labour is then the key to the interactive process (Marx would have said dialectical) by which men and nature fashion each other.

> 'Labour is, in the first place, a process in which both man and Nature participate, and in which man of his own accord starts, regulates, and controls the material reactions between himself and Nature. He opposes himself to Nature as one of her own forces, setting in motion arms and legs, head and hands, the natural forces of his body, in order to appropriate Nature's production in a form adapted to his own wants. By thus acting on the external world and changing it, he at the same time changes his own nature. He develops his slumbering powers and compels them to act in obedience to his sway' (*Capital*, vol. I, in McLellan, 1971:148).

It is a further consequence of Marx's theory that the relationship between the development of the productive forces, and the 'needs' which he continually refers to man as satisfying through them, is also a dialectical one. That is, 'consciousness of his own needs is a product of his historical development and attests to the cultural values achieved by preceding generations' (Avineri, 1968:79). This idea is a familiar one, reflected in the problems which arise in trying to arrive at a sociological definition of poverty. People's feelings of deprivation cannot be related to any absolute standard of living. It rests on the conception which they have of the minimum income necessary to maintain themselves in the way they feel they have a right to expect, and these expectations can only be derived from their (sub-) culture. Deprivation can only be expressed in terms of *relative* deprivation, and the standard for comparison will be drawn from the meaning-system of the particular social milieu in which the individual lives. Paradoxically, the growth of what is nowadays called the affluent society by no means assures general contentment.

> 'A noticeable increase in wages presupposes a rapid growth of productive capital. The rapid growth of productive capital brings about an equally rapid growth of wealth, luxury, social wants, social enjoyments, thus, although the enjoyments of the worker have risen, the social satisfaction that they give has fallen in comparison with the increased enjoyments of the capitalist, which are inaccessible to the worker, in comparison with the state of development of society in general. Our desires and pleasures spring from society; we measure them, therefore, by society and not by the objects which serve for their satisfaction. Because they are of a social nature, they are of a relative nature' (*Wage Labour and Capital*; MESW: 84-5).

In this way, Marx equips his theoretical system with an inbuilt dynamic element which will account for social change. Marx does not profess to tell us what specific organisational forms change will take, or prescribe inescapable 'laws' of historical development, as he is sometimes represented. What he is saying is that the impulse to initiate change, which supplies the ideas and the motivation to act, is a constant factor in human history. It arises from man's necessary and inescapable relations with nature, and shows itself in historical guise as a continuous improvement in the capacity of the productive forces to free people from existential cares. Each decisive phase of this advance, by the terms of Marx's theory, elicits a corresponding response both in terms of social organisation and an increase of knowledge.

A politically subordinate and economically exploited class is the human agent of change at the end of each epoch. For Marx, these descriptions were synonymous, and it follows from his discussion of the interrelationship between the institutional orders of society that this should be so. But he held a reverse relationship also to operate. That is to say, a class which became dominant in the sphere of production and exchange must succeed in bringing political institutions under its control. It follows, then, that from the collision between a degenerating and an emerging, dynamic system of productive organisation there crystallises a political struggle culminating in the displacement of the ruling class. In this way, class conflict supplies an answer to the question of why particular forms of society come into being and then recede into history. But conflict is also progress, since Marx sees each new epoch as marking a new and higher level in the development of the productive forces. The passing of epochs is likewise progressive in the special and more compelling sense that Marx believed that the cycles of social decay and new birth he identified in history (his work is bespattered with gynaecological imagery) had reached its final stage in the contemporary bourgeois world of which he was so close an observer. The revolution which overthrew the power of capitalism would be the last of its kind, for it would end class divisions and exploitation and so allow people to realise their human potential to live as free, creative beings. At the last, that is to say, a powerful and enticing millenarian vision dominates Marxian social theory.

Capitalism

Capitalist productive relations entail the capturing of political power by the bourgeoisie: that is what capitalism means. As Marx and Engels put it in the deceptively offhand remark in the *Communist Manifesto*, 'Each step in the development of the bourgeoisie was accompanied by a corresponding political advance of that class' (MESW:37). It is tempting, but very misleading, to read into this statement an implied analytical disjunction between economic and political power. On the contrary, it is intended to express their necessary interdependence. Marx's views on the relationship between the political order and private property in the means of production have tended to trouble sociologists considerably — probably much more than they should have done. Conceptually, at least, this relationship is clear enough. Class struggles are always, by definition, fought out on the political level. The central tenet of the materialist conception of history is that the attack which finally overthrows the political institutions of a ruling class is engineered by a class whose interests lie in establishing a new and incompatible system of social and economic organisation. It is this fact which sharply separates revolutions from mere power struggles. But from its first appearance as an organised entity, the revolutionary class of the future reflects the political weakening of the old order. Even within the compressed and polemical context of the *Manifesto* space is found to sketch out the emergence of the bourgeoisie as a political counterpoise for centralising monarchies against the feudal aristocracy. Nascent capitalism, again by definition, made its entry on to the historical stage *outside* the political economy of feudalism, most notably in the commercial cities of northern Italy in the fourteenth century. In the case of England, which Marx discusses in some detail in *Capital*, the triumph of bourgeois political institutions at the end of the seventeenth century was the culmination of a long, slow process of change which had begun with the development of agrarian capitalism in the fifteenth. Bourgeois political revolutions, therefore, ratify and complete in law and constitutional theory changes in social organisation which ultimately derive from the exhaustion of a particular mode of production. Whether this viewpoint can be defended is, of course, quite a different matter. The point is that nothing is gained by befogging the issue with chicken-and-egg questions about whether economic or political power 'comes first'. In the Marxian canon classes are political conflict groups; but their relationship to the means of production is what explains their emergence as collectivities mobilised for such conflict.

Many of the difficulties in reading Marx stem from the fact that he constantly moves backwards and forwards between an abstract model of capitalist development and historical illustration without ever signalling the fact. This procedure is inherent in the model itself, which treats class struggles in terms of social process, and specifically discounts the possibility of analysis in the static terms of social structure. The abstract model, Weber was later to observe, is a form of ideal-typification, and in a general way this is true. That is, 'capitalism' as a social system is a logical fiction culled from the study of more than one society. It is Engels, for once, who makes the telling point, in a footnote to the 1888 English edition of the *Manifesto*, when he says that

> 'Generally speaking, for the economic development of the bourgeoisie, England is here taken as the typical country; for its political development, France.'

Marx developed the underlying idea at some length in his critique of the American economist Carey:

> 'He belongs to a country in which bourgeois society has not developed from a background of feudalism, but began of its own accord; a country where this society was not the surviving result of centuries of development, but the starting point of a new movement; where the state, unlike all other national structures, was from the start subordinated to bourgeois society and bourgeois production, and could never pretend to a purpose of its own; where, finally, bourgeois society itself, linking the productive forces of the old world with the gigantic natural terrain of the new, has developed hitherto unknown dimensions and freedom of movement, and has far exceeded previous efforts to overcome the forces of nature, and where the contradictions of bourgeois society themselves only appear as transitory phenomena. It is not surprising that the production relationships in which this immense new world has developed so surprisingly quickly and fortunately are considered by Carey as the normal, eternal conditions of social production and distribution, contrary to what has taken place in Europe, especially in England — which for Carey is the real Europe — where the production relationships have been hindered and disturbed by the inherited obstacles of the feudal period' (McLellan 1973:59-60).

All the essential ideas on the relationship between state and civil society are present in this important statement. In the *18th Brumaire of Louis Bonaparte* Marx actually portrays a situation in which the state has become to some degree detached from bourgeois interests, as a result of a stalemate in the class struggle. This had occurred because the working class (which in France, according to Marx, had progressed much further than the English proletariat along the road of political struggle) had shaken bourgeois rule, but was not strong enough itself to assume power. In his search for a class ally, therefore, Bonaparte paradoxically represented himself as the champion of the peasantry, to which capitalism in fact holds out nothing except the promise of certain extinction. In view of the crude charges of 'economic determinism' which have sometimes been brought against Marx, it is important to insist on his very flexible application of the idea of class struggle in the analysis of actual capitalist societies. In the abstract model, the relationship between the state and civil society is analytically a very tight one, and unquestionably the links between property and the state give capitalist states an unmistakable social character. But it is also a character with — on another level of comparison — striking variations deriving from their unique historical and cultural evolution.

'Civil society' was a phrase current in Marx's day, and the distinction between the state and civil society expresses the alienation of private-property relationships. Civil society, Marx observes in *The German Ideology*, is a term which

> 'emerged in the eighteenth century, when property relations had already extricated themselves from the ancient and medieval community. Civil society as such only develops with the bourgeoisie. . . . Through the emancipation of private property from the community, the state has become a separate entity, alongside and outside civil society; but it is nothing more than the form of organisation which the bourgeois are compelled to adopt, both for internal and external purposes, for the mutual guarantee of their property and interests' (MECW vol. 5:89-90).

Bourgeois society completed the separation between state and civil society, by elevating to the status of natural law the right of individuals freely to dispose of private property in the means of production. Feudal and ancient societies acknowledged restrictions on this right in law, custom and religion, and the control of property imposed a reciprocity of rights and duties between master and servant. When Marx wrote most of his work, in the middle two decades of the nineteenth century, the state did indeed appear as 'a committee for managing the affairs of the whole bourgeoisie'. *Laissez-faire* social and economic prescriptions, especially in England, ruled untrammelled. The political franchise was restricted to substantial property owners, and the prime duty of government was defined as non-interference in the economic life of the society, except insofar as its force was necessary to support the capitalist class in its dealings with refractory workers. For Marx, it only multiplied the irony that capitalism had created the juridically free worker. This freedom, for the proletarian, is only the sham, legalistic obverse of the freedom which the bourgeoisie claims for itself to appropriate for private use the wealth which is socially created, without social responsibility. Expropriated from the means of production, the proletariat is free only to sell its labour to capitalists in order to exist. This is the basis of the class struggles which destroy the capitalist mode of production.

Bourgeois law shows up with unusual clarity what is common to the polity in all epochs: that it is a social mechanism by means of which the ruling class 'pumps out' (Marx's phrase) surplus value from the producers of wealth. The state is a parasitical excrescence on the life of civil society, and political power ('properly so called') nothing but the capacity of one class to dominate another, an instrument of exploitation. But capitalist industrialism exhibits the qualities generic to class societies in intensified form. As the *Manifesto* puts it, 'for exploitation veiled by religious and political illusions, it has substituted naked, shameless, direct, brutal exploitation' (MESW:38). Every social transaction acquires its price, and for the individual under capitalism 'both his power over society and his association with it is carried in his pocket' (McLellan 1973:77). The rights he has are not those stemming from membership of a community, but those he can buy through hiring out his labour-power. The warmth and spontaneity of human relationships is supplanted by the cash nexus. Capital reigns, not merely as a productive system, but as culture, creating its own mean, crabbed, life-denying morality:

> 'Its true ideal is the *ascetic* but *usurious* miser and the *ascetic* but *productive* slave. Its moral ideal is the *worker* who takes part of his wages to the savings bank. . . . Its principal thesis is the renunciation of life and of human needs. The less you eat, drink, buy books, go to the theatre or to balls, or to the public house, and the less you think, love, theorise, sing, paint, fence, etc. the more you will be able to save and the *greater* will become your treasure which neither moth nor rust will corrupt — your *capital*. The less you *are*, the less you express your life, the greater is your *alienated* life and the greater is the saving of your alienated being. Everything which the capitalist takes from you in the way of life and humanity, he restores to you in the form of *money* and *wealth*' (Bottomore 1963:171).

Alienation is an overarching concept in Marx's work from first to last, although it makes only brief appearances in his shorter, more circumstantial writings. He uses the idea to express the perception that society, which could and should be the outcome of man's free and creative relationship to nature, constantly appears to the individual as an alien, constricting and hostile force outside himself. The antithesis of alienation is freedom, and predictably, therefore, Marx discerns in the state the institutional embodiment of an alienated existence. The bourgeois class itself is corrupted and malformed by the brutal scramble for profit, but retains the misshapen resemblance of humanity. The proletariat lacks even this resemblance. The notion of alienation also provides a consistent, contrasting theme to the triumphs of technological progress, especially under the rule of the bourgeoisie. Although the means to create freedom from want and enriched leisure are brought to a high pitch of development with the progress of epochs, the proletarian masses know only degradation and despair. Marx argues for the messianic role of the proletariat in the historical process precisely in terms of the lunatic contrast between the cumulatively more successful organisation of societies to fulfil their needs and the progressively more intolerable social conditions which each successive mode of production imposes on most members of society. Under capitalism, alienation is total and universal; and what appear in the initial stages of the class struggle as the purely economic aims of the proletariat end as an assertion of the right of every individual to live a life of dignity and release from material deprivation. The idea central to alienation, then, is the distortion of human relationships. Society creaks on only as a system of forced labour and political repression designed to protect the privileges of a few.

However, alienation is much more than a linking concept in Marx's evolutionary scheme. As always, he looks to the real, sensuous world of human activity for the working out of historical processes, and alienation has its most basic form in the mundane experiences of the proletarian at work. The intensive division of labour which is a feature of capitalist productive relations reduces the worker to simply one more factor of production, and his job to mindless slavery. But, Marx proclaims in a famous passage in *Wage Labour and Capital*,

> 'the exercise of labour-power, labour, is the worker's own life-activity, the manifestation of his own life. And this *life-activity* he sells to another person in order to secure the necessary means of *subsistence*. Thus his life-activity is for him only a means to enable him to exist. He works in order to live. He does not even reckon labour as part of his life, it is rather a sacrifice of his life . . . . On the contrary, life begins for him where this activity ceases, at table, in the public house, in bed' (MESW:75).

Furthermore, the product of the worker's labour-power is appropriated by the bourgeoisie in the form of surplus value. The essence of the capitalist market is the production of commodities for exchange, not for use, and hence the growth of money as a medium of exchange:

> 'The necessity of exchange and the transformation of the product into a pure exchange value progress to the same extent as the division of labour, i.e. with the social character

> of production. But just as exchange value grows, the power of money grows too; that is, the exchange relationship establishes itself as a force opposed to the producers, and independent of them. What was originally a means to the furtherance of production becomes a relationship alien to the producers' (McLellan 1973:72).

Money presents itself to the worker as the social power of the ruling class over him, in the form of accumulated labour-power — capital.

Each of these forms of alienation expresses an aspect of the powerlessness of the worker, and is linked with the division of labour, a term which, Giddens (1973:88) suggests, Marx used in two complementary ways which he did not distinguish very carefully. In the first case, the alienation of the worker takes the form of self-estrangement, and is the outcome of the rationalising techniques inherent in capitalist production which turn him into an automaton. In its second meaning, the division of labour refers to the existence of classes and the exploitative relation between those who dispose of wealth and those who produce it. Alienation must therefore remain until the division of labour (in both senses) is transcended, together with the class system of capitalism. This culmination of Marx's argument is the source of endless (and unresolved) problems of interpretation. He considered that scientific (as opposed to utopian) socialism must recognise the inescapable necessity of using advanced industrial technology as the basis of a hitherto undreamt-of material abundance, but gave virtually no clue as to how the sweeping away of private property in the means of production could resolve the problems of industrial organisation and political control (see Giddens 1973:89-91). The fact that Marx used the expression 'transcendence' rather than 'abolition' in respect of both the state and the division of labour as they appear after the destruction of capitalism is important as exonerating him from counter-accusations of mere utopianism. But the fact remains that the forms of this transcendence are never made clear.

Alienation exists, finally, as ideology, as alienated ideas, which have their most universalistic formulation in religious world-views:

> 'The basis of irreligious criticism is this: *man makes religion*; religion does not make man. Religion is indeed man's self-consciousness and self-awareness so long as he has not found himself or has lost himself again. But *man* is not an abstract being, squatting outside the world. Man is *the human world*, the state, society. This state, this society, produce religion which is an *inverted world consciousness*, because they are an *inverted world*. Religion is the general theory of this world, its encyclopedic compendium, its logic in popular form, its spiritual *point d'honneur*, its enthusiasm, its moral sanction, its solemn complement, its general basis of consolation and justification. It is *the fantastic realization* of the human being inasmuch as the human being possesses no true reality. The struggle against religion is, therefore, indirectly a struggle against *that world* whose spiritual *aroma* is religion.
>
> *Religious* suffering is at the same time an *expression* of real suffering and a *protest* against real suffering. Religion is the sigh of the oppressed creature, the sentiment of a heartless world, and the soul of soulless conditions. It is the *opium* of the people.
>
> The abolition of religion as the *illusory* happiness of men, is a demand for their *real* happiness. The call to abandon their illusions about their condition is a *call to abandon a condition which requires illusions*. The criticism of religion is, therefore, the *embryonic criticism of this vale of tears* of which religion is the *halo*' (Bottomore, 1963: 43-4).

The point of this frequently misunderstood claim is not that the ruling class deliberately fosters religious belief in order to procure obedience and submission from those it exploits. It may certainly have that effect, by explaining and justifying the human predicament in terms which obscure the real causes and remedies of suffering. But the illusions are *shared* illusions. The whole power of religion over men's minds stems from the fact that the conditions of their material existence obscure the workings of the natural and social world from them. It is in this sense that Marx and Engels (in *The German Ideology*) insist that,

> 'The ideas of the ruling class are in every epoch the ruling ideas: i.e. the class which is the ruling *material* force is at the same time its ruling *intellectual* force. The class which has the means of material production at its disposal, consequently also controls the means of mental production, so that the ideas of those who lack the means of mental production are on the whole subject to it' (MECW vol. 5:59).

The phrase 'means of mental production' is somewhat ambiguous, but the general import of the passage is plain enough. Through its control over the formation and dissemination of ideas, the ruling class propagates ideals and values which express and legitimate its own particular mode of domination; aristocracies, for example, give pride of place to virtues such as honour and loyalty, the bourgeoisie to freedom and equality. However, ideology in Marx's definition must be sharply disengaged from the notion of political propaganda. As in the case of religion, Marx asserts that ruling-class ideologies are not to be confused with consciously constructed myths to deceive the lower orders. On the contrary, in their origins these ideas are *revolutionary*, the ideational forms in which an emergent ruling class mobilises against the old in the name of the 'general' interest. The bourgeoisie, in the prime of capitalist ascendancy, are the inheritors of a belief-system which to them is natural, right and eternal, like the society they rule. But the power of these ideas over society at large necessarily crumbles as changes in the material base renew the class struggle. As the *Manifesto* has it, the precondition of revolutionary ideas is a revolutionary class. It follows, on the other hand, that history is not to be understood as a series of pitched battles between classes, and periods of stability are not to be explained in terms of unadorned coercion. Class-divided societies can and do rest on shared values; but common values are themselves a consequence of ruling-class power. The will of the ruling class shapes institutions and culture in the service of its dominant mode of production.

Underpinning the whole imposing structure of bourgeois power is the mechanism through which the capitalist appropriates surplus value from his workers. The central mystery to be resolved was how the insertion of the capitalist market between the producer and consumer created exchange value (money) over and above the cost of production; this could never be the case, for example, in a feudal economy based on subsistence agriculture and purely local needs. For an answer, Marx turned not to an examination of the operation of the market itself, but to the labour theory of value. Stripped of its tortuous accretions, this theory holds that the exchange value of commodities is fixed by the number of units of labour-power required for making them. To arrive at the definition of a unit of labour-power involves arguments of dreadful complexity which are of no concern here. The point is that although Marx recognises that the problem of supply and demand on the market is a crucial one for his theory, he solves it (by means of the notion of 'socially necessary labour-time') to his own satisfaction. The effect is to leave intact his contention that labour alone creates the value of a commodity, expressed as its price (this argument is taken from Robinson 1949: 10-15). The whole secret of the accumulation of capital, therefore, lies in the fact that labour itself becomes a commodity to be bought and sold. The capitalist pays his workers less value than they produce for him during the working day, wages being only the expression of the value which they consume themselves. The difference between the two prices is surplus value: 'surplus', that is to say, in the special sense that it is the product of 'surplus labour far beyond the worker's requirements. . . . far beyond his immediate needs for the maintenance of his livelihood' (McLellan 1973:100). In another idiom, surplus value is bourgeois profit, but the difference in terminology is also one of intent. Marx's analysis holds out the possibility of establishing a just, non-exploitative price for labour. Furthermore, if only labour creates value, then by definition the ownership of private property in the means of production, which is accumulated past labour, is parasitical. The amazingly powerful productive forces released by capitalism, conversely, are created *by* the bourgeoisie, but *at the expense of* the proletariat, within a system of exploitation more universal, more efficient, and more complete than in any previous epoch.

As so often, Marx stresses what is unique to bourgeois industrialism rather than what is common to all class societies. *The German Ideology* draws a quite radical distinction between 'natural instruments of production and those created by civilisation' (MECW vol. 5:63), and therefore between agrarian and industrial economies. The feudal ruling classes, for example, were tied to the communities over which they exercised jurisdiction by the nature of their property. Through their common dependence on the land, both lord and labourers experienced some degree of mutual subordination to the life of the cooperative community. With man-made means of production – machinery – the case is quite different. For the first time in human history, the means of production offer the possibility of creating a massive labour surplus. But manufacture also presupposes an extensive division of labour, the development of the market and a money economy, and all that is implied by the phrase 'industrial revolution'. This revolutionising of the means of production totally transforms all social relations. Workers relate to each other only as competitors in the labour market. Their lives are controlled by the machine – objectified labour – in a double sense: in terms of physical constraints and also because every operation of the machine creates more surplus value for the capitalist, which reinforces his domination of labour. By the same token, however, large-scale industry smashes all vestiges of patriarchalism, which gave earlier epochs some semblance of a social, therefore human, existence. To the capitalist the worker is an instrument of production, like the machine, useful only insofar as he increases capital. The bourgeoisie itself is the first ruling class in history to push exploitation to its extreme, logical conclusion, through a total withdrawal from involvement in the productive life of the community. Marx, who was well aware of the tendency toward the separation of ownership and control in industry, regarded this as the culmination of monopolistic greed:

> 'It reproduces a new financial aristocracy, a new variety of parasites in the shape of promoters, speculators and simply nominal directors; a whole system of swindling and cheating by means of corporation promotion, stock issuance and stock speculation. It is private production without the control of private property' (*Capital*, in Avineri 1968:178).

It is also the precondition of the constitution of the bourgeoisie as the first truly *national* ruling class. Unlike the feudal estates, the bourgeoisie have no local particularistic interests, the growth of capitalism was itself coeval with the rise of the nation-state. Its mode of production demanded the pacification and extension of the political community, to provide markets; the destruction of all inherited privileges which could form an obstacle to commerce and the utilisation of capital; and the apparatus of centralised administration appropriate to such a gigantic enterprise. Moreover, capitalism has ceased to be even a purely national phenomenon. The *Communist Manifesto*, in particular, is full of the imagery of capitalism militant, employing all the resources of an advanced technological society to 'batter down Chinese walls' through trade and conquest. There is, therefore, no irony in the statement that 'The bourgeoisie, historically, has played a most revolutionary part'.

Despite his many strictures on capitalist iniquities, in fact, Marx was second to none in his undisguised admiration for the vigour and ingenuity of a class which first forged mass societies characterised by political and economic centralisation; and then burst through national confines to make its own history world history.

From the point of view of the social theorist, the bourgeois epoch lays bare the laws of development and change in society which point the way to the communism of the future. The separation of ownership and control, for instance, not only demonstrates with a completeness no argument can match the moral indefensibility of bourgeois property relations; it also presages the social control of associated producers over their own labour. In a fashion mutilated by greed and human misery, the bourgeoisie have given notice of the immense productive forces which 'slumber in the lap of social labour'. Their slogans of equality and freedom, although ideological lies, foreshadow a vision of true equality and freedom. This is the essence of the dialectical progress of societies, in which each epoch is devoured by the class antagonisms it engenders, without sacrificing what is positive in mankind's achievements. The 'cunning of reason', in Hegel's phrase, which guides human development, is revealed by the capitalist mode of production – but in its active, material form of a class struggle to end exploitation and alienation on behalf of all humanity. History does not make itself, it is made by men. The last great contribution of the bourgeoisie to progress, therefore, is the revolutionary proletariat.

Conflict and Revolution

The capitalist mode of production is unique in that it rests upon a continuous and accelerating process of technological and social innovation:

> 'The bourgeoisie cannot exist (the *Manifesto* declares) without constantly revolutionising the instruments of production, and thereby the relations of production, and with them the whole relations of society. Conservation of the old modes of production in unaltered form was, on the contrary, the first condition of existence for all earlier industrial classes. Constant revolutionising of production, uninterrupted disturbance of all social conditions, ever-lasting uncertainty and agitation distinguish the bourgeois epoch from all earlier ones. All fixed, fast-frozen relations, with their train of ancient and venerable prejudices and opinions, are swept away, all new-formed ones become antiquated before they can ossify. All that is solid melts into air, all that is holy is profaned, and man is at last compelled to face with sober senses his real conditions of life, and his relations with his kind' (MESW: 38).

Competition for markets is the fundamental and necessary principle underlying this perpetual social tumult. The bourgeoisie is united against the proletariat but divided against itself. During phases of industrial and political expansion the consequences of competition for endogenous change are masked, although every increase in the power of capital is dependent upon swelling the ranks of the proletariat. Nevertheless, the condition of capitalist survival is success in competition, and Marx sees clearly that the logical end of the system is the formation of monopolies through the destruction of rivals: 'one capitalist always kills many'. The fact of bourgeois competition determines the behaviour of capitalists as individuals quite independently of their personal predispositions. The humane and enlightened members of the class must accept the standards set by the most ruthless and rapacious, or be overwhelmed.

Capitalism also intensifies the rate of exploitation through the introduction of machinery. This is true both from the point of view of a comparison of epochs, as earlier noted, and in the sense that technological innovation produces a leap-frogging effect, as capitalists attempt to outdo each other through the construction of more sophisticated means of production:

> 'Like every other advance in the productivity of labour, machinery is to cheapen commodities, and to diminish the part of the working day in which the worker works for himself while increasing the part of the working day which he gives to the capitalist for nothing. Machinery is a means for producing surplus value' (Marx 1930:391).

It does so by multiplying the power of the human body through mechanical means. From the very outset, the development of mechanical means of production leads to the alienated reversal of the normal conditions of human labour, in that 'The worker's activity, limited to a mere abstraction, is determined and regulated on all sides by the movement of the machinery, not the other way round' (McLellan 1973:155). Not merely is human craftsmanship obliterated, but the operative himself becomes a frail extension of the means of production. The effect upon the price of labour, moreover, is catastrophic. In a specific, but very revealing, illustration of his general thesis, Marx observes (1930:418 ff.) that women and children can now compete with men for work. The market levels all distinctions of age and sex, and competition invades the 'private' sphere sacrosanct in hypocritical bourgeois morality — the family. 'In former days, the worker used to sell his own labour power, being ostensibly in this respect, a free person. Now he sells his wife and his children. He becomes a slave trader' (Marx 1930:420). The minimum price of labour power is determined by the needs of the family, the reproductive unit of future generations of workers. Where once the single worker earned the reproductive subsistence for the whole family, all its members now sell their labour for that same subsistence, with a corresponding leap in the rate of appropriation. The capitalist, driven by the fear of obsolescence of his plant, seeks to exploit it continuously through night-working and the prolongation of the working day. Given the natural and political limitations on this procedure, he also tries in every way possible to speed up the machine and, eventually, to replace it with a more efficient one. Marx actually opposes to the term 'manufacture' that of 'machinofacture'. Manufacture demands a division of labour, but as its etymology implies, the product is still that of the worker's hand and brain; he is not yet an appendage to the machine. Furthermore, Marx suggests, manufacture developed as a response to a shortage of labour, in order to meet the demands of new markets. The whole purpose of machinofacture, on the contrary, is to *replace* the worker, to overcome the limitations imposed on productivity by the weak human frame. And it does so, with the effect of creating what Marx calls an 'industrial reserve army' of unemployed, thus swinging the market for labour heavily in favour of the employers (Marx 1930:469 ff.). Corresponding to the breakneck enlargement and concentration of capital, therefore, is the immiseration of the proletariat.

The development of bourgeois industrialism (again, in contrast to earlier epochs) drastically simplifies the class structure. Smaller concentrations of property are swallowed up by competition, and the petty-bourgeois stratum absorbed within the proletariat. The peasantry dies out following its dispossession from the land, and appears either as industrial wage-labour or joins the lumpenproletariat in the great cities, that intriguing collection of hucksters, pimps and mountebanks which Marx describes in *18th Brumaire* (MESW:138). Empirically, Marx frequently acknowledges the existence of a more complex class order than the dichotomous scheme for which he is famous, and which is essential to the idea of conflict. But the trends immanent in the formation and concentration of capital mean that, for all practical purposes, the bourgeoisie inters every class except the one necessary to its survival, the proletariat. Observe an important point here therefore: if one asks how many classes there are under capitalism, no simple answer emerges. It all depends whether Marx is using the abstract model or discussing specific class formations.

The industrial working class itself becomes increasingly undifferentiated, since improvements in machine technology eliminate the social distance and conflicts of interests previously separating the artisan 'labour aristocracy' from machine-minders. Furthermore, the dramatic leap in the creation of surplus value makes possible an economy based partly on luxury and conspicuous consumption, and the conditions of the two antagonistic classes diverge so sharply as to separate them into 'two nations', as Engels phrased it in *The Condition of the Working Class in England*. The degradation and humiliation of the proletariat is the condition of pampered sloth for its exploiters, and Marx, in a footnote to *Capital* (1930:478), notes without comment the cruel paradox revealed by Engels who 'shows how pitiful is the condition of many of these workers who are engaged in the production of luxuries'. As the capitalist epoch reaches its zenith, therefore, the deprivation and exploitation of the proletariat lead to combinations of workers against owners, and so to the organisational and ideological foundations of class solidarity. Initially, working-class action often takes blind and irrational forms of protest, such as machine-breaking; it ends with the proletariat setting up its own political associations. At the point where the working class has articulated its interests in opposition to capital, and is organised politically to fight for them, Marx speaks of the *class-for-itself,* which term is used in contrast to *class-in-itself*. A passage from *The Poverty of Philosophy* illustrates the basis of this distinction:

> 'Economic conditions had in the first place transformed the mass of people into workers. The domination of capital created the common situation and common interests of this class. Thus this mass is already a class in relation to capital, but not yet a class for itself. In the struggle, of which we have indicated only a few phases, the mass unites and forms itself into a class for itself. The interests which it defends become class interests. But the struggle between classes is a political struggle' (MECW vol. 6:211).

The same distinction appears in Marx's sketch of the French peasantry in *18th Brumaire*:

> 'The small-holding peasants form a vast mass, the members of which live in similar conditions but without entering into manifold relations with one another. Their mode of production isolates them from one another instead of bringing them into mutual intercourse. . . . In so far as millions of families live under economic conditions of existence that separate their mode of life, their interests, and their culture from those of other classes, and put them into hostile opposition to the latter, they form a class. In so far as there is merely a local interconnexion among these small-holding peasants, and the identity of their interests begets no community, no national bond, and no political organisation among them, they do not form a class' (MESW:171-2).

The capitalist mode of production, on the contrary, forces the proletariat into solidary action. Although from one point of view workers are in competition with one another, their common interest in the maintenance of wages in the face of an increasing rate of exploitation unites them against capitalists, at first on the local level, and then nationally. Bourgeois industrialism thrusts masses of workers into large-scale factory and urban settings, subjecting them to brutal conditions in the search for profits. In such social environments, communication and combination are made easy. Marx evidently attributed especial significance to the workplace in this respect. The proletariat (wage-labour) is definitely distinguished from 'the poor' in a general sense. The conditions of life of the lumpenproletariat, the *Manifesto* notes, prepare it not for revolution but to become the 'bribed tool of reactionary intrigue'. It is in the process of conflict with the bourgeoisie that proletarian consciousness has its origins. The bourgeois ideology of legitimation crumbles under the impact of the social reality which workers experience in their daily existence, and this proletarian 'education' is further catalysed by the social and political mobilisation of the working class to support the interests of one national bourgeoisie against another, as in wars for colonial supremacy. Marx derives enormous relish from the thought that capital in this way necessarily provides the conditions for the growth of the class which will overthrow it. It is also one of the most powerful elements in his theory, in that he traces the demise of the bourgeoisie to changes emanating from an inherently unstable structure of social relations.

During the course of the protracted struggle, proletarian class consciousness far outleaps its merely economic interests. Although they are rooted in the division of labour, classes do not come into conflict over the division of wealth: still less are they groups earning different incomes. The proletariat attacks the bourgeois economic system first obviously, because this is its most immediate and pressing experience of capitalist domination. 'But the struggle between classes is a political struggle', because Marx can see no possibility of any compromise of interests. The clue to the impossibility of a truce situation under capitalism lies in the nature of its competitive imperative, 'expand or die'. The point of revolutionary conflagration, according to Marx, cannot long be postponed beyond the critical moment when the capitalist market collapses as a consequence of its own world-wide domination.

The power of capital vanishes as its outlets for its products dry up, and a series of progressively more severe economic and social crises ensue in the capitalist world. By a neat touch, Marx links these crises of overproduction with the ruthless exploitation of the proletariat which is the foundation of bourgeois domination. Overproduction occurs not in the sense that society's needs are satiated, but because the spending power of the working class is deliberately sacrificed to capital accumulation. The argument is in certain respects incomplete, but the evidence as its stands,

> 'suggests that Marx intended to work out a theory on some such lines as this: consumption by the workers is limited by their poverty, while consumption by the capitalists is limited by the greed for capital which causes them to accumulate wealth rather than to enjoy luxury. The demand for consumption goods is thus restricted. But if the output of the consumption-good industries is limited by the market, the demand for capital goods is in turn restricted, for the constant capital of consumption-good industries will not expand fast enough to absorb the potential output of the capital-good industries. Thus the distribution of income, between wages and surplus, is such as to set up a chronic tendency for a lack of balance between the two groups of industries' (Robinson 1949:48-9).

So, then, the toppling of the bourgeois state is explained ultimately in terms of the imbalance between production and consumption, revealed in the choking of capitalism's distinctive social institution, the market. It is now that the bourgeois epoch enters the phase of extreme contradiction, which for Marx is always the prelude to political revolution: contradiction, that is, between bourgeois social relations and the further development of the productive forces to satisfy human wants. The proletariat develops its revolutionary aims and organisation with every step in the enfeeblement and disarray of the bourgeois ranks, until its force overthrows the rights of private property, and with it the last class society in history. The last word on this amazing theoretical *tour de force* can most appropriately be left with Marx himself, in a confident and apocalyptic mood which returns us to the themes of conflict and progress with which the chapter began:

> 'This antagonism between modern industry and science on the one hand, modern misery and dissolution on the other; this antagonism between the productive powers, and the social relations of our epoch, is a fact, palpable, overwhelming; and not to be controverted. Some parties may wail over it; other may wish to get rid of modern arts in order to get rid of modern conflicts. Or they may imagine that so signal a progress in industry wants to be completed by as signal a regress in politics. On our part, we do not mistake the shrewd spirit that continues to mark all these contradictions. We know that to work well, the new-fangled forces of society, they only want to be mastered by new-fangled men — and such are working men. They are as much the invention of modern time as machinery itself. . . . To revenge the misdeeds of the ruling class there existed in the Middle Ages, in Germany, a secret tribunal, called the *Vehmgericht*. If a red cross was seen marked on a house, people knew that its owner was doomed by the *Vehm*. All the houses of Europe are now marked with the mysterious red cross. History is the judge — its executioner, the proletarian' (McLellan 1971:208).

2 The cage of the future: Weber

With Weber we enter a thoroughly politicised world. As Giddens (1973:46-7) puts it, 'At the risk of some oversimplification it can be said that, whereas Marx's abstract model of capitalist development proceeds from the "economic" to the "political", Weber's model is derived from the opposite process of reasoning, using the "political" as a framework for understanding the "economic".' This statement can be given more precision by pointing to the critical part played by Marx's prediction of the breakdown of the capitalist market in undergirding his entire theory of proletarian revolution. The effect of this prediction is to specify definite structural limits within which the capitalist class can act successfully to buttress its rule by political cunning. In the long run, the bourgeoisie is helpless to prevent the erosion of its social control by forces which its own mode of production sets in motion and cannot reverse. Since Weber rejected this account of the necessary evolution of capitalism, he was compelled to approach the problem of social order from the opposite direction, by exploring the scope and limitations of the methods of social control available to any ruling group. We can put it like this: Weber's social theory raises to a point of central importance the ruling strategies of cajolery and coercion which Marx had treated comparatively superficially, because he regarded them as being in the last analysis irrelevant to the stability of capitalism.

Weber both modifies Marx's view of capitalist development and moves beyond him to a more general model of industrial societies. In complex, highly differentiated social structures of this type (he reasons) power falls to those who can create and control the administrative and decision-making machinery essential to the planning and integration of social activity. The development of bureaucratic administration is, for Weber, the organisational precondition of the emergence of the large-scale, centralised nation-state. The bureaucracy is a formal organisation uniquely fitted (compared with previous methods of administration) to the control of complex, territorially large, and socially heterogeneous political communities, because its impersonal, rule-bound, standardising procedures expedite great volumes of variegated business. Since an increasingly intense regulation of social life is all that makes such states possible, Weber cannot share Marx's optimism about a socialist future where the constraints of directives are replaced by the free co-operation of all the citizens. On the contrary, 'socialism would in fact, require a still higher degree of formal bureaucratisation than capitalism' (Weber 1968:225), because of the greater emphasis on planning and control by the state.

The development of bureaucratic administration endows the state with great stability. This stability derives chiefly from the ability of rulers to shape social processes through administrative control and interference. There is also the more sinister possibility, that these sophisticated methods of social control may be applied for repressive ends. Weber insisted that the state 'even more than other institutionally organised communities, is so constituted that it imposes obligations on the individual members which many of them fulfil only because they are aware of the probability of physical coercion backing up such obligations' (Weber 1968:903). The state can and will use force against recalcitrant groups — in fact, the successful enforcement of a monopoly of physical coercion is what, for Weber, defines the state in the first place. It is important to bear this in mind, because Weber is sometimes mistakenly represented as emphasising the element of legitimacy in social control (cf. Dahrendorf 1958:166). This is misleading both in fact and in intention, since Weber's whole point is that any social order will be explicable in terms of varying mixtures of consensus and coercion. The state is uniquely and peculiarly the agency which disposes of the resources for coercion within a given territory. It is the repository of the most drastic means of exercising power, which Weber defines as 'the probability that one actor will be able to carry out his will despite resistance, regardless of the basis on which this probability rests' (Weber 1968:53). As Bendix (1966:290) remarks in an illuminating aside, this is 'very similar to Clausewitz's definition of war.' It is also, as Weber himself was the first to point out, too encyclopaedic as a definition to have much analytical value. It covers all social situations, from dyadic interaction to relations between societal groups such as classes; and a whole gamut of coercive tactics, of which physical compulsion would constitute only one extreme form. Weber therefore chose to work, in the context of his political sociology, with the concept of 'domination'. (He habitually employs two words, *Macht* and *Herrschaft*, either of which might reasonably be translated as 'power'. The only important thing is to distinguish between them for analytical purposes, and the present discussion follows the usage of Roth and Wittich in the only full translation of *Economy and Society* at present available in English. They render *Macht* as 'power' and *Herrschaft* as 'domination'.)

Domination is 'the probability that a command with a given specific content will be obeyed by a given group of persons' (Weber 1968:53). At this point, like 'power', 'domination' is defined as a purely factual relationship between social actors. It is already, however, more manageable. It incorporates three important elements. (I am here following the excellent discussion by Bendix (1966:285-97) of Weber's basic concepts in political sociology). There must be a group of rulers who issue commands on the assumption that they can influence or enforce obedience; these commands will vary in content; and therefore will also be designed to bring varying social groups to compliance. It is now that we are in a position to talk about large, impersonal systems of societal regulation. Such systems require what is called by Weber a 'staff' — a political apparatus to execute and enforce commands on behalf of rulers. We are thus led back to the problem of *administration*. 'We are primarily interested in "domination" insofar as it is combined with "administration". Every domination both expresses itself and functions through administration' (Weber 1968:948). Always Weber insists that every extended system of domination has to be understood in terms of a three-way relationship between rulers, enforcing officials ('staff'), and the ruled. Then, to this bare definition he adds the crucial sociological rider that domination 'implies a minimum of voluntary compliance, that is, an *interest* (based on ulterior motives or genuine acceptance) in obedience' (Weber 1968:212). It is probably this statement as much as any other which has led people to credit Weber with a one-sided emphasis on legitimacy as the source of social cohesion. Rather confusingly, however, the minimum of *voluntary* compliance he insists on as being integral to domination is not the same thing as *willing* compliance. He uses the word, in fact, to distinguish analytically those situations where a social actor has no reason to resist a command, or refrains from resisting out of self-interest, including the self-interest which arises from the wish to avoid coercive action by the authority. Weber makes this clear more than once. For example, 'In a concrete case the performance of the command may have been motivated by the ruled's own conviction of its propriety, or by his sense of duty, or by fear, or by "dull" custom, or by a desire to obtain some benefit for himself' (Weber 1968:946).

Once through the dusty definitions, we find that Weber is offering us what might be termed — slightly tendentiously — an *inertia* theory of political power. This is somewhat misleading in that Weber emphasises cohesion and decisive action as the key to domination of the masses by an elite. They do not rule by doing nothing. However, bureaucratic administration provides a technically indispensable means of translating will into effective action. No matter how disaffected they may be, the ruled are helpless unless they are able to organise in their turn:

> 'The predominance of the members of [bureaucratic] structure of domination rests upon the so-called "law of the smallest number". The ruling minority can quickly reach understanding among its members; it is thus able at any time to initiate that rationally organised action which is necessary to preserve its position of power. Consequently it can easily squelch any action of the masses threatening its power so long as the opponents have not created the same kind of organisation for the planned direction of their own struggle for domination' (Weber 1968:952).

Weber then uses this perception to think systematically about non-rational motivations to obedience. The stability of a social order is founded not just on self-interest, legitimation, or the 'divide and rule' principle. The availability of sanctions in fact creates a frame of mind which obviates their use. Citizens may grumble about this and that, but as isolated individuals they do not see what can be done to change the situation. Sheer unreflecting *habit* becomes a widespread motive for compliance. What begins as resentment and frustration often ends as apathy and resignation, because the personal cost of kicking against the traces is too high. Marx sees revolutionary class conflict at the heart of capitalist political economy. Weber believed that the principles of social organisation underlying the technological triumphs of capitalism had also immeasureably strengthened the possibilities of stable political control. Weber does not deny class conflict, nor that it may under certain circumstances take on revolutionary forms. What he does suggest is that the odds are heavily against it. To repeat, it is certainly wrong to label Weber as a consensus theorist. It is, perhaps, not unfair to say that he is the theorist of political quietism.

In many respects Weber endorsed Marx's sociology of capitalism, as well as his detestation of it. It might have been Marx who wrote that, 'whereas the physical whip assures the exertion of slaves locked in barracks. . .the wage whip and threat of joblessness guarantees the effort of the "free" worker' (Weber 1968:1010). For Weber, however, the future is obscure and promises no happy ending:

> 'No one knows who will live in this cage of the future, or whether at the end of this tremendous development new prophets will arise, or there will be a great rebirth of old ideas and ideals, or if neither, mechanised petrification, embellished with a sort of convulsive self-importance. For of the last stage of this cultural development, it might be truly said: "Specialists without spirit, sensualists without heart, this nullity imagines it has attained a level of civilisation never before achieved"' (Weber 1958: 182).

This 'cage of the future' is the bureaucratised, centralised state which represents a constant and increasing threat to individual freedom. There is a prevalent misconception (recently repeated by Swingewood 1975:151) that Weber equates bureaucratic administration with political control by bureaucrats, an idea popularised in the notion of 'rule from Whitehall'. This is not true. Bureaucracy supplies an indispensable element in domination (through *expertise*) but is itself being used for a variety of political ends. Underlying the process of bureaucratisation itself, however, is what Weber calls 'the disenchantment of the world'. By this he means the *rationalisation* of all social life which has been characteristic of capitalist development and of Western European culture generally:

> 'The more organised and rational society is, the more each of us is condemned to what the Marxists of today call alienation — condemned to feel that we are enslaved by a whole which is greater than we are, condemned to realise only a share of what we might be, doomed to perform all our lives a limited function whose prime merit and nobility lies in the acceptance of those very limitations' (Aron 1970: vol.2, 249).

The opposite of 'freedom' in this sense, then, is not physical coercion but something akin to that sense of individual bewilderment and futility which Durkheim and Marx express through the concepts of anomie and alienation. Like Marx,

Weber was a committed political activist, believing that only through the struggle to keep great ideals alive is change possible at all. He stood closer to the powerful than Marx could or wanted to. But he could never elude the pessimism of his scientific studies, which suggested to him that the instrumental ('disenchanted') ethic of capitalism, combined with its technical efficiency, will buy it uneasy but long-term peace at the expense of a culture which, from a humanistic point of view, is dead. Weber would have thoroughly approved of Tawney's observation that we live in a society whose slogan is 'Produce! Produce!' but which can never give an answer to the question 'Produce for what?'. Insofar as socialism abandons the self-critical pursuit of individual freedom in favour of 'growth' it can only lead to the same sad end.

Weber makes very explicit what is perhaps deducible from but unstressed in Marx's writings: that the expropriation of the worker from the means of production is only a particular case of the expropriation of the means of administration and thus of the means of exercising power. It follows, then, that the economic power of capitalists, based on private ownership of large-scale property, is only one historically specific form of the appropriation of material resources which always accompanies any system of domination. Marx certainly did not follow through the implications of such a formulation. Late in his life he lambasted Bakunin for suggesting that the administrators of 'collective' property would themselves create a new basis for domination; 'idiocy', Marx called it. Marx never dealt with the problem of how capitalist technology could be freed from its system of authority relationships, nor by what mechanisms 'political power properly so called' (the capacity of one class to oppress another) could be replaced by the 'administration of things' in the general interest, despite his hints of participatory democracy (Giddens 1973:90,279).

Classes, Status Groups and Parties

Classes, status groups and parties are 'phenomena of the distribution of power within a community'; 'they presuppose a larger association, especially the framework of a polity'

(Weber 1968:927,939). Power, therefore, is not to be understood as a separate 'dimension' of inequality (see Parkin 1972:46; Giddens 1973:44). Classes, status groups and parties are the collectivities through which power is mediated and expressed. The Weberian triad can be usefully seen as in a sense corresponding to the economic, ideological and political aspects of capitalist power identified by Marx (see Swingewood 1975:140-6). Weber, however, insisted on making rigorous conceptual distinctions between the three types of formation, precisely as a means of attacking what he viewed as certain inflated claims made by historical materialism. His argument was that the economic, social and political orders, although obviously related in any process of social change, are nevertheless autonomous spheres of social action, none of which is reducible to the other. They only influence each other in various ways according to specific constellations of circumstances. At the same time, in the concluding pages of *The Protestant Ethic and the Spirit of Capitalism*, Weber was at pains to emphasise that he regarded his work as complementary, not antithetical, to the materialist conception of history. Despite their very considerable differences on the level of explanation, Weber agreed with Marx that capitalism is what Miliband has neatly christened a 'business civilisation'. It is a form of society in which the *ad hoc* and adventitious means of creating wealth are replaced by the rationalised, continuous and essentially planned exploitation of the market. There is, for example, a very great deal in Weber's writings that parallels Marx's discussion of the emergence of civil society, and this fact helps account for some obvious resemblances between the two of them in their analysis of capitalism.

Despite this last remark, it is essential to notice immediately that what for Marx constitutes the essence of 'class' — its engagement in a political struggle — Weber firmly excludes from his own definition. He treats classes as strictly economic groupings, in the sense that their social action is directed to the market for goods and services, either to satisfy needs or to make a profit. The existence of classes thus depends on the operation of a market for commodities or labour — under capitalism, the price of labour is the central issue between classes. Slaves, Weber points out, are not a class but a negatively privileged status group, according to his own terminology. Capitalism, on the other hand, *is* a class society in the double sense that 'it vastly extends the range of market operations beyond that characteristic of prior forms of society; and that it is a system based upon the relationship between capital and "free" wage-labour' (Giddens 1973:51).

Weber defines a class (1968:302) as quite simply 'all persons in the same class situation'. He also severely restricts the meaning of class interests (Weber 1968:928-9), to connote, not the interests of a class as a collectivity, but the interests of individuals arising from their class situation. This is a purely operational decision, and anyone is entitled to use these terms in the way that best answers his theoretical requirements. The point for Weber is that class interests cannot then be confused with class consciousness, which involves social action by members of one class in relation to another, as opposed to mere 'mass action' among members of a class. The individual's class situation 'derives from the relative control over goods and skills and from their income-producing uses within a given economic order' (Weber 1968:302). Such control differentiates life chances as determined by the market. The possession of property, Weber agrees with Marx, is a fundamental arbiter of life chances, but he will not accept the propertied/propertyless dichotomy as exhausting the range of class situations and thus of class interests. This is a crucial point of theoretical departure, and opens up the way (among other things) for the analysis of the non-propertied 'middle' classes under capitalism. For the market chances of the propertyless may be themselves highly differentiated, because of important differences in access to the skills and qualifications needed to win advantage in the labour market. This part of Weber's analysis corresponds to Marx's concept of the class-in-itself, nevertheless, since it is concerned only with the factual inequalities generated by the market, and implies nothing about the likelihood or specific forms of class action.

While such an approach is clearly suited to reflecting

the complexities of the capitalist market, it clearly is of very little assistance in suggesting objectively identifiable lines of demarcation within which the sociologist might expect to discover patterns of social differentiation linked with the hierarchy of class. Weber therefore now introduces the term *social class*, which he defines as 'the totality of those class situations within which individual and generational mobility is easy and typical' (Weber 1968:302). The criterion of blocked mobility is a crucial one, for it demonstrates that a social class has succeeded in establishing something of a monopoly over resources which confer advantages in the market, such as private property, or educational opportunity. Now, therefore, it becomes possible to speak of class stratification, not merely of class inequality, since differences in market chances are inherited. A social class, then, is formed by a process of closure.

'The status group', says Weber somewhat cryptically, 'comes nearest to the social class' (Weber 1968:307). This is one of the rare occasions when Weber in any way abates his harping on the conceptual antinomy between 'class' and 'status' stratification. The link between them lies in the process of closure, since we are also told that status stratification is under way wherever we find 'consensual action of a closing character' (Weber 1968:932). 'Status group' and the medieval 'estate' are both translations of the German *Stand*, which later came to be applied to the superior strata in German society (Bendix 1966:85). This underlines Weber's own point that status-group formation can only be understood in relation to the distribution of power within a given community. Like classes and parties, status groups are interest groups, although the interests they pursue are not those of economic acquisition or the pursuit of power, but ideal interests. To make it clearer just what Weber meant by this, it is helpful to look briefly at his argument in *The Protestant Ethic*. In that book he is concerned to demonstrate that any explanation of the rise of capitalism in terms of class interests alone can only be achieved by robbing the concept of class interests of all useful meaning. The spirit of capitalism, far from being the ideological creation of an emergent bourgeoisie, was the unintended outcome of the smashing of the religious hegemony of the Catholic church at the Reformation. Calvinist theology in particular, and Protestantism in general, prescribed for its adherents a worldly asceticism which demanded a systematically ordered life of religious devotion in which *work* had a prime ethical significance. Thus, Weber reasons, key ideational ('ideal') components of the capitalist ethos were originally propagated by an other-worldly theocracy. The fact that Protestantism found favour with the growing bourgeoisie, and gave purpose and justification to their secular pursuits, is neither here nor there. The development of such a world view must be allowed an irreducibly autonomous place in the analysis of capitalist development, because the specific forms taken by Calvinist theology and pastoral practice cannot be regarded as in any sense derived from material or political interests. Insofar as Protestants pursued these ends (and of course they did), it was as part and parcel of other, transcendent ends which gave meaning to their lives. And for Weber sociology as a science was dependent on the elucidation of such systems of meaning.

Two general observations about the concept of 'status group' are appropriate at this point. First, Weber clearly intended its use to reflect the restricted utility of 'class' and 'class interests' as the basis of group solidarity and action. He insisted not only that cleavages based on (for example) race or religion are a reality *sui generis*, but observed that they have dominated pre-industrial stratification systems to such a degree as to repress the emergence of a market such as capitalism demands (Weber 1968:937). The knightly estate and the Brahmin caste are two examples illustrating the point. They highlight the opposition between class and status stratification, for in the societies they rule the pursuit of economic gain through exchange in the market is ethically stigmatised. Weber therefore argues (1968:304) for a radical distinction between 'class' and 'status' societies, which he considered to be fatally obscured by Marx's assumption of a generic similarity between all societies deriving from the exploitation of labour-power. Status societies, for instance, create economically irrational patterns of consumption, and confer monopolies on specific groups which hinder the free exchange of goods and services in the market. 'Class' and 'status' are therefore antithetical *principles* of stratification. Where the market plays a minimal or subordinate part in the allocation of life chances it is pointless to speak of a class society. The 'pure' status order recognises only *personal* attributes as the basis of inequality; the 'pure' class order acknowledges as legitimate only those differences which arise from the *impersonal* operation of the market. It is against the broad background of Weber's crusade against the over-simplifying propensities of historical materialism that his nagging insistence on the analytical distinction between class and status must be judged. A great deal of this insistence arose from Weber's interest in pre-industrial societies, an interest which is of only tangential relevance here.

However, Weber extended the meaning of 'status group' to refer to an ideal-typical collectivity which embraces 'all instances of cohesive social groups with their subcultures and exclusion of outsiders' (Bendix 1966:85). The process of social closure by co-religionists draws attention to the defining (ideal-typical) feature of the status group. This type of collectivity (unlike the other two) is the 'bearer' (to use Weber's own word) of a distinctive system of values, which enjoins upon its members both a particular way of life and the rejection of outsiders as unworthy of fellowship. Hence the notions of 'style of life' and 'social honour', which constantly crop up in the context of Weber's discussions of status. 'Way of life' is perhaps a better phrase than 'style of life' these days, since contemporary usage has tied the latter expression too closely to patterns of consumption. Weber evidently meant to refer to the different meaning and use of wealth in his remark that classes are stratified according to the principles of the acquisition of goods, status groups according to principles of consumption (Weber 1968:935). Religious movements in general provide some notable instances of ideal interests as the basis of social bonding, but the conceptual deployment of the concept of status group is by no means confined to the sociological study of religion.

On the contrary, it is only where one group acquires domination over another that we can begin to speak of the status situation as 'every typical component of the life of men that is determined by a specific, positive or negative, social estimation of *honor*' (Weber 1968:932).

In one extreme case, this control may operate only on the purely individual social level, in the form of exclusion or ostracism. At the other pole, the social dimension of stratification may be a means by which one group permanently excludes the members of another (either individually or collectively) from any share of political and economic power. For obviously the principle underlying status-group formation – social closure – can serve these kinds of interests as well. In fact, in a statement which for Weber has an unusually categorical ring, we are told that

> 'material monopolies provide the most effective motives for the exclusiveness of a status group; although, in themselves, they are rarely sufficient, almost always they come into play to some extent' (Weber 1968:935). (Quite clearly Weber here has in mind the operation of *privileged* status groups.)

On an empirical, rather than a conceptual level, in fact, Weber readily concedes that equality of status coexists only precariously with property differences, and notes the 'extraordinary regularity' with which property is recognised as a status qualification. The same sort of link also operates between status groups and political, as opposed to economic, power. Patterns of intermarriage and sociability, for example, are means by which political control can be restricted to a circle of like-minded people. Indeed, social closure by elite groups is integral to any system of domination, which must always decide in principle what sort of people are to be allowed access to the means of power. An examination of Weber's account of how a ruling minority retains supremacy in a complex, bureaucratically administered society shows that it does so in part because of its unusually cohesive *social* qualities – the 'law of the smallest number'. Without assenting to historical materialism as he understood it, then,

Weber constantly showed himself ready to accept the close congruence between the economic, social and political aspects of stratification as an historical fact.

Interestingly, Weber's definitely ambivalent attitude on this question is reflected in a certain definitional shuffling of which he does not seem to have been aware. That is, the overall tendency in his writings is to treat the status group as an ideal-typical 'community' in the sense indicated above. However, at certain points, he also quite explicitly refers to status groups as collectivities which successfully lay a claim to superior prestige within a community (Weber 1968:304-5). What appears to be missing that could link these two ideas, Parkin points out (1972:41), is some acknowledgement that those who control the means of economic and political power also have in their hands the sources of ideological hegemony, as in Marx's 'ruling class — ruling ideas' thesis. The root of the problem, however, is less in Weber's indifference to the question than in his compulsively circumspect answer to it. Assent to Marx's view in a general way is entailed by Weber's insistence on domination as the central concept in the analysis of social order, and his observation (Weber 1968:213) that every system of domination tries to legitimate itself. Weber even went further. He agreed that one source of prestige was the appropriation of political and hierocratic power (Weber 1968:305). There is also no doubt that Weber saw the legitimation of a social order as being in some degree assured by sheer longevity of domination, which in turn (he suggested more than once) was connected with the stable distribution of economic power. However, he could not be more explicit about the relationship between class power and ideological control precisely because it might foreclose issues concerning the role of values in social change which *The Protestant Ethic* was written to keep open. But at the very least, it does no violence to Weber's fussy sense of exactitude to interpret him as saying that the normative dominance of elites is usually in evidence, if only by virtue of their power to suppress and deflect oppositional world views. Here lies the link with what have become more or less standard definitions of status groups, as 'clusters of people occupying similar levels of prestige', and so on. Insofar as the disprivileged accept their subordination as legitimate, and defer to their superiors, society can be conceptualised as a hierarchy of prestige. However, such deference is necessarily an empirical matter, not one of definition. Unfortunately, it is 'status group' in the sense of 'prestige group' which has been seized upon, and usually in a trivialised way at that. In this sense, the term has little analytical value, and an understanding of Weber's position in relation to Marx's theory depends critically on appreciating the significance of his methodological warning that to 'treat "class" conceptually as being equivalent to "community" (*Gemeinschaft*) leads to distortion' (Weber 1968:930).

Having established a rigid *conceptual* distinction between class and status stratification, Weber stresses that class position is a frequent basis for communal action. Moreover, he points out (Weber 1968:935) that 'today the class situation is by far the predominant factor' in status-group formation. He merely wishes to be clear that they are not co-terminous. A common class situation is only one among a potentially very large number of social characteristics which may be the basis of that sense of community singled out by Weber as the hallmark of the status group.* For Marx, the developing struggle between capital and labour ultimately pushes all other distinctions into the background. The significance of 'status' is that it is designed to draw attention to the existence of cleavages and conflicts which cut across social class divisions, or alternatively reinforce them. Contemporary South Africa is an outstanding case in point. In the context of that society it makes little sense to speak of the working class as an entity, because its white fraction stands in a politically and economically privileged position with respect to blacks. In South Africa, therefore, there exists a much stronger tendency for market struggles to be translated into power

* In this instance, the terminology of Gerth and Mills, in *From Max Weber*, is more suggestive than that of Roth and Wittich in *Economy and Society*. The latters' rendering of 'status groups are normally groups', is very unhelpful. It also misses the crucial symmetry of the contrast between classes, which are not definitionally communities, and status groups, which are.

struggles, since any claim for a 'fairer share' threatens the political institution of apartheid and the doctrine legitimating it. Northern Ireland is a case of a somewhat different kind, being properly understood as a nationalist conflict for which religion provides the major institutional focus. Both these examples deal with collectivities whose social action cannot be rendered intelligible in terms of class interests and allegiances. It is to cope with the empirical analysis of just such types of inter-group conflict that Weber chooses to define status groups, rather than classes, as characterised by the 'subjective awareness of solidarity' among their members (Giddens 1973:80).

The idea of status groups is also obviously designed to express Weber's dissatisfaction with the way in which some versions of historical materialism conflated a number of meanings of 'class consciousness'. It is possible, Mann suggests (1973:13), to identify at least four different usages of the phrase in Marx's writings, all the way from awareness of class identity to purposive revolutionary action. Marx had never found it necessary to discriminate very carefully between these usages, since his theory aims to demonstrate the linkages between them. Weber, on the contrary, insisted that even the organised pursuit of market interests could by no means be expected to follow from the experience of inequalities, unless given a push by politically active minorities; and he mentions the intelligentsia as one important mobilising influence on working-class perceptions.

Weber is, however, very sceptical about the development of a strong sense of community within the working class as a whole. He does go a considerable way with Marx. In capitalist societies work, and therefore occupational success and its attendant material and symbolic rewards, lies at the core of the dominant meaning-system. The class order is thus invested with a moral meaning which other types of society have not attached to the existence of material inequalities. Under capitalism, the facts of class inequality are not held up as part of the natural and inevitable ordering of the world. On the contrary, the individual's class position is represented as an expression of his innate capacities, which can be transformed through personal endeavour. Unlike the status societies of the Middle Ages and Antiquity capitalism has evolved a value-system in which the constraints and deprivations of class frequently bring the disprivileged into collision with these values. Moreover, in contrast with other types of society, capitalism encourages class-conscious organisation, because it puts large numbers of people into the same class situation and concentrates them at the workplace. It also exposes them to the uncertainties and fluctuations of the market for labour in a fashion wholly unlike the local economies of pre-industrial societies. The exigencies of the capitalist class order have thus produced communities of work and living which are the basis of solidarism. Not only do working-class people marry each other and go to the pub together, but they have developed a distinctively collectivistic value-system. When Mrs Morel (in *Sons and Lovers*) banged the poker in the grate of her back-to-back house as a sign that she needed urgent help from her neighbour, she symbolised a tradition of mutual aid among many working-class communities which was developed to cope with a hard and precarious existence. In this sense, the working class has some of the qualities of a status group. However, Weber (1968:932) distinguishes between the strong and weak ('amorphous') form. In the weak form, we may infer, people are conscious of the superficial social resemblances between themselves and others, but are not bonded by a coherent ideology common to the group. Weber sees the emergence of a class-for-itself, Marx's revolutionary community, as highly improbable. Only rarely does the working class act as a class (for instance, in general strikes), and then with only limited political aims. As many writers after Weber have pointed out, capitalism has created not so much a working-class community as many working-class communities.

Why so? Weber gives a number of reasons. For instance, 'Mobility among, and stability of, class positions differs greatly; hence the unity of a social class is highly variable' (Weber 1968:302). Not only has a large middle class interposed itself between the propertied elite and the alienated machine-minders envisaged by Marx, but the working class

Weber viewed as being itself frequently in competition internally, for example between skill-levels and industries. It is too huge, too physically scattered and too socially heterogeneous to develop that discipline and purpose needed to translate numbers into social power. Both the possibility of upward mobility and competition for higher wages weaken class unity. Then again, Weber suggests, the sheer complexity of the market system often obscures the understanding of cause and effect, so that class action does not spill over into political radicalism as means to ends. This particular issue is of course inseparable from that of the manipulation of normative consensus through a dominant meaning-system; but it is very characteristic of Weber's insistence on the complex interplay between fact and value that he should pause to consider how confusing the world appears from the horizon of the factory bench, and how disorderly the 'facts' to which any radical ideology must appeal.

It certainly cannot be said, on the other hand, that Weber ever composes these scattered observations into anything resembling a critique of Marx's theory of proletarian revolution. Weber's projected excursion into this theoretical field was never even begun. He did however lay particular stress on the fact that any successful political action by the working class would be conditional upon its creating a party, or attaching itself to an existing one. A 'party' is a formal organisation which holds itself ready to influence social action, irrespective of the particular issues on which this influence is brought to bear. It can exist at many levels of social structure, but the classical form of the *genus* is for Weber the mass, bureaucratised party of the modern era. Classes and status groups affiliate themselves in various combinations to parties (Weber 1968:938), and from one angle it is useful to think of them as furthering the interests of these groups. However, parties also work to stimulate and articulate interests which might otherwise remain latent. They can, conversely, act as a brake upon political action, because parties depend for their existence on full-time staffs organised in a bureaucratic hierarchy to a large degree, even though the principle of elective offices makes them somewhat unlike the governmental apparatus of control. As such, parties tend to develop interests of their own, a theme taken up later in the discussion of Michels' work. In general, Weber stresses the difficulty of making any very useful generalisations about the interaction of classes, status groups and parties outside of a specific historical context, since they react upon each other in empirically very complex ways.

Status and Prestige

Notice that 'status group', in the sense of a prestige group, necessarily loses its ideal-typical character. Everything turns on there *in fact being a more or less agreed-on prestige order*. A prestige 'level' can only be a summation of individual judgements, based on the rankings which people assign to themselves and others. A prestige order cannot rest on invidious social distinctions because it entails acceptance of common values which, while creating honorific discriminations, bind the members of a collectivity into a community. This is most easily observed in small groups or local communities (interactional status systems) in which ranking is the subject of personalised evaluations. For some sociological purposes it is important to know that such prestige rankings exist. The application of the principle uncritically to the capitalist class order, on the other hand, leads to conceptual muddles and no empirically useful results. The concept of a single, uniform prestige order implies a consensus of values. In effect, then, a subordinate prestige group cannot be a conflict group, because unless there is a high measure of agreement about the characteristics which confer prestige, several hierarchies of ranking will emerge, not one. There are, and have been, societies which approximate the type. Capitalism is not one of them, precisely because its dominant ethos is one of competitive individualism; which, furthermore, is in perennial tension with the factual operation of a market dominated by private property. This, combined with the peculiarly favourable structural conditions for united class action which industrial organisation creates, makes conflict between classes a notable and permanent feature of capitalist social organisation.

The view that there is indeed a hierarchy of prestige acknowledged equally by all the classes has been given a certain currency by studies of occupational prestige rankings. A glance at the ordering of these rankings shows that they closely parallel the factual distribution of class advantages. Furthermore, it is also broadly true that respondents at all levels of the class order tend to reproduce the same pattern of ranking. The trouble with all these studies, however, is that they have invariably been grounded in what Parkin (1972:40) calls the moral referendum approach to prestige. If all the individual assessments are turned into a composite score for an occupation, then 'consensus' is bound to result as a matter of arithmetical necessity. It is possible in this way entirely to overlook the systematic discrepancies in ranking between classes, such as are reported by Young and Willmott (1956) among manual workers. They found that a class-conscious minority actually reversed the overall pattern of ranking, reflecting a coherent set of counter-values which placed the greatest social usefulness and prestige on manual work. A more common mode of 'deviance', noted by other researchers too, is the elevation of the respondent's *own* occupation in the prestige scale, notwithstanding an assent to the lower status of manual work generally. There is other evidence, too, that working-class respondents forcibly reject implications of status derogation. Well known surveys carried out in America around 1940 asked people to identify themselves with the upper, middle or lower classes. Between 79 percent and 88 percent said they were middle class. The finding was hailed in some quarters as incontrovertible proof of the advent of middle-class America. Centers repeated the experiment, but substituting 'working class' for 'lower class' He found that 80 percent of manual workers were quite happy to put themselves in that category (Centers 1961: 30-1,85-7).

The more their design is studied, moreover, the less is it clear what exactly occupational prestige rankings really rank. It is usually assumed, for instance, that the respondents in such studies are capable of disengaging the concept of 'prestige' from the other more mundane, but quite relevant, attributes of occupations. Turner's (1958) effort to get his respondents to disentangle the strictly personal, moral evaluations from judgements of 'public opinion' about occupations, turned up a very complex state of affairs not hinted at by the neat ordinal tables which other rankings produce. As a matter of fact, the most ambitious and widely-quoted study of occupational prestige actually imported the word 'prestige' illicitly into the title. The National Opinion Research Centre's study of 90 occupations, carried out in 1949 and replicated in 1963, asked people their opinion of the 'general standing' of the jobs (Hodge *et al.*, 1966:323). The grounds for inferring that this is the same thing as prestige remain a mystery to this day. Speaking in more general terms, it simply makes no sense from a scientific point of view to see that the occupational order and prestige rankings correlate closely, and then to allege that it is prestige which is really at issue. Occupational prestige rankings, as so far developed, are not so much wrong as completely meaningless. The consensus they reveal is not moral but practical, the preference for one type of job rather than another, about which there is likely to be a good deal of agreement. Still less can they be adduced as evidence of consensus on values in a more fundamental sense. Wide-ranging questions of social and political attitudes cannot be reduced to such a constricting quantifiable methodological format. To give a single, simple instance: why stop at the evaluation of what are conventionally regarded as occupations? Why not ask people to rank 'Someone living in very considerable luxury off an unearned income'? The results would undoubtedly inject a little more interest into occupational rankings, and also dispel the illusion that the occupational order and the class structure are synonymous terms, as seems often to be assumed.

Lastly, and in some ways this is the most decisive objection of all to prestige rankings, it should be noted that the tendency to conceptualise the structure of inequalities in prestige terms is itself a class-related phenomenon. Dahrendorf (1959:280-9) long ago pointed out that researchers working independently of one another found that the less privileged were much more likely to have an image of society founded on power, and expressed as a fundamental divide between 'us' and 'them'. These contrasting modes of perception are, of course, polar types. An empirically more common mode of variation is the extent to which money and possessions, rather than 'breeding', education and family background are mentioned as the criteria of class assignment. Centers (1961:98-9) found that,

> 'It is noteworthy that members of the upper and middle classes more commonly think of education as a reason for membership in the middle class than working and lower class people do. . . . A similar statement might be made regarding family, position and environment. They seem much more important to middle and upper class people than to others, and rank just after education with them.
>
> To the members of the working class the most important criterion of membership after money and income is the ownership of a small business, profession or trade; in sum, being an independent operator or proprietor of some kind.'

In other words, there is a clear tendency among working-class people to emphasise the brute facts of class inequality at the expense of those symbolic aspects which are conventionally supposed to confer superior prestige. Prestige models of society, on the other hand, are very much the supportive ideology of those having the material security to devote themselves to status striving in an effort to legitimate their good fortune. To think of the social order in terms of a continuum of prestige positions is a natural construction of the privileged, and one which would have surprised Weber no more than Marx.

Marx and Weber

Where then does all this leave us — what generalisations can be distilled about the application of the Weberian triad to the analysis of class in capitalist societies? In the strictest sense — and one feels it might have appealed to Weber's hankering after conceptual precision — perhaps the answer should be 'none'. Even so, a very cursory general comparison of Marx and Weber is useful, because they complement each other's strengths and weaknesses.

Marx's historical imagination has a very urgent sweep, and he sees social processes in terms of the progress of whole epochs. Nonetheless, his work, where it was not of an essentially philosophical and speculative character, centred upon the inner workings of capitalism. On the most abstract level, Weber was concerned to question the idea that Marx's model of capitalist development could be applied to pre-industrial social systems in a creative way. Furthermore, in his insistence on political and ideological aspects of power as autonomous modes of social change, Weber wished to underline the point that the relationship between the economic and other institutional orders in society is a contingent one. Bourgeois capitalism, with its political domination by propertied interests, the free market, and liberal-democratic freedoms, is only one of the possible combinations of particular forms of technological organisation with a 'superstructure'. Even within the capitalist camp wide variations are discernible. To point out the obvious contrast, both Japan and Germany were transformed industrially by traditional, not bourgeois, elites (Moore 1966). Neither developed strong indigenous forms of political democracy. The United States, which did, also imported black slave-labour, and thus complicated the class system by overlaying it with a degree of status differentiation not really matched in Europe. Of course, the operation of private property interests and the labour market is bound to create broad similarities of social structure. But differences in political organisation, and the persistence of ethnic, religious and national differences within the capitalist states makes 'capitalism' far from monolithic in structure and development. Marx, of course, acknowledged such diversity, but did see these various forms of social differentiation as finally subordinate to the exploitative but faltering market, which imposes on the propertyless proletariat its specific liberating task. Since, as pointed out at the very beginning of this chapter, Weber cannot accept such a view, it follows that for him the significance of class conflict for social change shrinks dramatically. 'Class' is no longer the pre-eminent concept in the analysis of conflict and change, but becomes only one of the sources of collective consciousness and political action. This is true even of capitalism, in which the conditions for class-conscious organisation are exceptionally propitious.

However, something is also lost in Weber's writing, and that is the sense of the continuous development of capitalism as a particular form of social and economic organisation. Marx gives a brilliant account of that most improbable of circumstances — the unification of a disparate mass of isolated producers into a political force within a specific mode of production. Beside it, Weber's adversions to the ideologically limited and politically fragmented nature of class action under capitalism stand out for what they are — empirical commonplaces. But Weber has something else, a strong belly-to-earth perception of how things get done (or fail to get done) because the organisation is lacking to translate individual discontents and aspirations into action. His great contribution to the study of power is the recognition that the *means* by which it is exercised is not just a technical problem of linking decision to execution. Without the means of administration, there is no power. Those who control the permanent apparatus of administration, therefore, shape the lives of the unorganised mass, not least (if needs be) through repression. Even where organised political opposition is permitted, it can be successfully contained through the superior resources available to the officially accredited respresentatives of the political community. Unquestionably, Marx's own thoughts on the nature of power have been scandalously simplified, by friends as well as enemies (Swingewood 1975:ch.6). No doubt, too, we should discount Marx's more utopian allusions to the character of political regulation in the classless society of the future. It is impossible, however, to argue away the fact that Marx's discussions of the nature of the state and bureaucracy constitute a vast blank area in his theory. To borrow Koestler's simile, the struggle of two antagonistic classes, unmediated by the state machine on the one hand and by party organisation on the other, is like a two-storey house with no lift and no stairs. From one, restricted, point of view, the analysis of bureaucratic administration can be said to complete Marx's work by providing an account of the organisational mechanisms through which class domination is transmitted. But in a wider sense it is also an account of the conditions of unfreedom. Bureaucracy – whether in a capitalist or a socialist political order – is the means by which domination is routinised and made secure, so that men accept their fate as irremediable and thus 'natural'. Furthermore, social movements dedicated to the realisation of a different kind of society founder on their own need for organisation in the struggle for power. In this sense, as Giddens (1973:50) puts it, bureaucracy is 'escape-proof'. While Weber insisted on the essentially unforeseeable character of capitalist evolution, therefore, his view of the probabilities makes it fair to say that he goes halfway with Marx – the pessimistic half. His is a depressing vision of alienation without end. The tensions between these two very different perspectives on the future form the context within which to set the chapters which follow.

3 The end of ideology?

If there is one point on which sociologists reach instant and universal agreement, it is that capitalist societies have become progressively and most impressively richer. Some of them have also seen in the affluence of the postwar period reason to believe in the permanent abatement of class conflict. They stress the effect of new modes of institutional control, and new techniques and knowledge (especially Keynesian economic theory), in mitigating the cycle of boom and slump which has periodically threatened the stability of capitalism, and tend to prefer labels such as 'industrial' and 'post-capitalist' society as a means of signalling this break with the past. They argue that the development of administrative and technical skills makes possible a planned industrialism qualitatively different from the crude engine of unregulated entrepreneurial individualism. Institutionally this metamorphosis has been marked by the emergence of trade unions, employers associations, pressure groups, and the universal franchise, by means of which potentially conflicting groups can channel and reconcile their interests. It will be noted that knowledge and democratic institutions are the key to this balance, and together represent mechanisms for translating the struggle between social classes for power into the search for optimal solutions to the common problem of creating prosperity for all.

These are the 'end-of-ideologists' of whom Mann (1973:10) picks out Bell, Lipset and Kerr as the chief representatives. It must be said clearly, however, that the phrase is not particularly associated with any one person or body of theory. End-of-ideologism is rather an evolutionary perspective embedded in a number of empirical generalisations, which are summarily stated by Giddens (1973:283). Violent clashes between capital and labour have become less common, revolutionary party programmes have been progressively abandoned, the working class has dwindled in relative size, and union membership has tended to level out during the past generation. Although no systematic statement of the reasons for these changes is to be easily found the following distillation of logical components is a fair representation of the overall interpretation of processes of social change in this century:

1. Modern industrialism has transformed the conditions and composition of the working class. Further, structural changes in the occupational order have made for great upward mobility.
2. The state has not become merely a coordinating device for generating greater wealth, though it does indeed have this function. In addition, through egalitarian welfare and educational measures it has redistributed goods and services and promoted a more fluid interchange between classes.
3. Therefore, class conflict is securely locked within an overarching consensus which does not question the basic rules of the bargaining game.

Thus, for example, Lipset (1963:412-3) finds that the biggest problem facing the western democracies (though it is really America he has in mind) is that of over-much intellectual and cultural conformity. His vision is that of a nation at work to secure its collective future, not to mention that of the rest of the world. 'Class' struggle will continue, but in a highly domesticated and good-natured form, 'without ideologies, without red flags, without May Day parades' (Lipset 1963: 408). In the striking epigram coined by Kerr and his associates, memoranda will flow instead of blood.

It should also be emphasised that end-of-ideologists do not link affluence with the decline of class conflict in any crude way. Affluence, in fact, can really be as well interpreted as the effect as much as the cause of social consensus. The fashioning of institutions for the management of conflict is to be understood as reflecting a shift in the balance of power between the classes. Lipset, always the most unequivocal of the theorists here under review, has put it as follows:

> 'Representatives of the lower strata are now part of the governing groups, members of the club. The basic political issue of the industrial revolution, the incorporation of the workers into the legitimate body politic, has been settled' (Lipset 1963:92; cf. Marshall 1950).

The forces of the right and left, he argues, have met upon the middle ground of 'conservative socialism', because neither side has anything to gain from political extremism. The (assumed) ascendancy of governments over economic institutions opens the door, in the context of democracy, to an interpretation of political processes as the means by which political representatives acquire *legitimation* through open competition between interest groups. Power, in this analysis, becomes shorn of its Marxian association with class interests, because elections are conceived of as an institutionalised form of 'democratic class struggle'. Thus (the argument concludes), private-property ownership and the forces of the market are no longer of central relevance to the analysis of this type of 'industrialism'.

Obviously, this point of view raises very important theoretical issues. At the same time, it also involves some straightforward claims about the role of political agencies in shaping the reward system of modern western societies. At this point, therefore, it is useful to review some of the empirical work which has a bearing on such claims, in order to lay the basis for a critique.

Patterns of Inequality

An initial distinction is needed between 'income' and 'wealth'.

Income, while by no means an unequivocal term in itself, is usually thought of as taxable revenue. Wealth refers to those forms of property, such as savings, shares, real estate, businesses and suchlike, which only attract the attentions of tax commissioners insofar as they yield personal income during any given accounting period.

It would be generally conceded by all authorities that such redistribution as has occurred is small. Kolko states flatly that,

> '. . . the basic distribution of income and wealth in the United States is essentially the same now as it was in 1939, or even 1910' (1962:3).

Certainly Pen (1971:163-5) lends support to this as a general judgment. On the basis of figures for a number of countries he concludes that in this century the ratio of profits to labour, interest and land-rent has remained stable at around 1 : 4. Estimates of the concentration of wealth vary, and are usefully reviewed by Littlejohn (1972:112-4). The most modest suggests that the top 9 percent of the population control only (if that is the word) half the personal wealth in Britain, and there is no reason to believe that this situation is being progressively transformed. Although the proportion of income accruing to property has dropped sharply relative to labour in this century, Pen points out that this is to be expected, given the growth of the labour force itself, and the whittling away of small-scale ownership. Between 1955 and 1965, income from property increased by 134 percent, as against 84 percent for earned incomes (Hughes 1968). The distribution of income is remarkably similar in all the capitalist countries, especially in the proportion going to the bottom 30 percent of the population, and gives a faint inkling (but no more) of the staggering disparities in market power which these societies tolerate. Effective economic *control* is even more concentrated. In America in the early fifties 2 percent of shareholders held 58 percent of the stock, and 67 percent one-tenth of the stock between them. In Britain, at about the same time, 1 percent of the adult population owned 81 percent of the ordinary share capital of public companies (Kolko 1962:52; Allen 1966:152).

Table 3.1.1 Long-term trends in distribution of private property, 1911-1960 and 1961-1971, Britain

Groups within adult population (aged 25 +)owning stated proportions of aggregate personal wealth	Estimated proportion of aggregate personal wealth						
	Period 1911-1960 (common basis)					Period 1961-1971 (common basis)	
	1911/13 %	1924/30 %	1936/38 %	1954 %	1960 %	1961 %	1971 %
Richest 1% owned	69	62	56	43	42	32	26
Richest 5% owned	87	84	79	71	75	55	47
Richest 10% owned	92	91	88	79	83	*	*
Hence:							
Richest 1% owned	69	62	56	43	42	32	26
Next 2-5% owned	18	22	23	28	33	23	21
Next 6-10% owned	5	7	9	8	8	*	*
95% owned only	13	16	21	29	25	45	53
90% owned only	8	9	12	21	17	*	*

Note: The series for 1911-1960 cannot be compared with that for 1961-1971. Though the two series are both derived from information on death duties, the coverage and assumptions used differ between the two. As comparison between the 1960 figures of the first series and the 1961 figures of the second series suggests, the second series is likely to understate the degree of concentration of ownership while the first series probably overstates it.

* We have not calculated the proportions of property owned by the richest 10 per cent and the remaining 90 per cent for 1961 and 1971, as the data are in such a form as to make estimates of those figures more uncertain than the other estimates shown for these years.

Source: Westergaard and Resler 1975:112

Routh shows for Britain that manual workers have not altered their share of income relative to other earners during this century either. True, lower white-collar occupations have experienced a relative decline compared with workers and managers in industry. However, three cautionary points are in order. First, a more elaborate time series shows that a zig-zag progression is characteristic, leaving the skeleton of income differentials untouched. Secondly, middle-class incomes have a well-attested tendency to 'disappear' into the various forms of hidden benefit later discussed. Fringe benefits are very much a feature of recent decades in business

Table 3.1.2. Concentration of main types of private property, 1954, Britain

Groups within adult population owning stated proportions of the aggregate value of property of the kind indicated	Share of total within each of following categories owned by percentage of population specified on left				
	All net private capital %	Cash and bank deposits %	Land, buildings, trade assets %	Govt. and municipal securities %	Company stocks and shares %
Richest 1% owned	43	23	28	42	81
Richest 5% owned	68	48	58	71	96
Richest 10% owned	79	64	74	83	98

Source: Westergaard and Resler 1975:116

organisation. Last but not least, women are not included in the table. Women are worse paid in every occupational category, but discrimination intensifies with movement down the occupational ladder. For unskilled women, the pay was only a little more than half that of men. In the 'lower professional' category the proportion rises to 72 percent. Kolko likewise (1962:78) doubts whether gains in real income have benefited lower-paid groups more than others. The war helped them somewhat, but the subsequent 'affluent' era looks to have favoured the middle classes more, and this balance of probabilities applies to the British case too. At any rate, there is no element of special pleading in Routh's conclusion (1965:147) that, 'The outstanding characteristic of the national pay structure is the rigidity of its relationships.'

A popular slogan of the end-of-ideologist years was that affluence had replaced class poverty by case poverty. Yet at the height of the United States' postwar boom the Council of Economic Advisers drew up figures for their President relating to poverty, taking as their definition any family with an income of less than $3,000 a year. Even by this modest yardstick, they found that in the world's richest nation one-fifth of families were living in poverty. Predictably, old people figured heavily among the casualties. So too did non-white families, and those without a male head. What is really interesting, however, is just how far wide of the mark stereo-

Table 3.2 Occupational groups and male incomes, Britain, 1913-60

Occupational group		% rise in average earnings
1A.	Higher professionals	620
1B.	Lower professionals	546
2B.	Managers and administrators	925
3.	Clerical workers	689
4.	Foremen, inspectors, supervisors	898
5.	Skilled workers	804
6.	Semi-skilled workers	842
7.	Unskilled workers	849

Source: Routh 1965:104, table 47, adapted. Group 2A has been missed out, since it comprises mostly self-employed people, who present problems.

types of the poor are. The image of them as composed chiefly of the feckless unemployable, with large families, and living in urban slums, is contradicted by all the facts. Nearly one half lived in rural areas. 70 percent of them had one earner in the family, and 23 percent had two or more. Half had no children, and only 11 percent had four or more – about the national average (Atkinson ed., 1973:377-82). Speaking of Britain, a labour economist insists: 'The problem of workers with resources insufficient for their needs (defined as Supplementary Benefit rates) is not simply a problem of large families, of fatherless families or of ill-health. There are some male workers in full time employment in good health and with relatively small families whose earnings fall below this minimal level.' Significantly she adds that, 'Women workers have not been considered in this paper' (Marquand 1973:235).

Poverty *is* still class poverty, and it is merely glib to talk about mass affluence, not least because the working class bears the brunt of a deprived old age. The incidence of car-ownership is an instructive illustration of the point. The car is probably the most widely recognised symbol of affluence and 'middle-classness' in the popular imagination. The workers are rumoured to be forever (and successfully) lusting

Table 3.3 Shares in total personal income before tax, Europe, circa 1963

	% of population	
	top 10%	bottom 30%
Norway	24.9	9.8
Sweden	27.9	8.5
U.K.	29.3	9.3
Finland	32.5	5.9
Netherlands	33.8	8.2
France	36.8	4.8
West Germany	41.4	10.0

Source: Atkinson 1970:70

after new Mustangs and whatnot. The fact is that in Britain even comparatively menial and poorly-paid non-manual people have cars in proportions equal to those of skilled manual workers. This draws attention both to the lop-sided distribution of affluence and to something which is relevant to the general distinction between income and life chances. One of the notable characteristics of postwar capitalist economies is that they have been run to a large extent on credit. It is a commonplace that hire-purchase and finance companies like to lend to 'respectable' occupational groups, because their incomes, though often modest, are secure. In the case of house mortgages, even more, it is well understood that middle-class status is decisive in the decision to lend. There is a simple disbelief abroad among businessmen in the creditworthiness of manual workers over long periods of time. And they should know. What is most remarkable about working-class consumer affluence is not so much its extent, as the sneering incredulity to which it has given rise among people who see it as a symbol of status-striving. This in itself is evidence of the strong in-built moral associations which any form of property-ownership carries among the relatively privileged. There exist deeply ingrained prejudices about what is appropriate for various levels of society, which make it difficult for those who feel vaguely affronted by working-class affluence to understand that (in Lockwood's neat dictum) 'a washing machine is a washing machine is a washing machine'.

Table 3.4 Proportion of Households and Persons in Those Households Owning Cars: by Social Class 1966, England and Wales (percentages)

Social class	With no car		With 1 car or more	
	Households	Persons	Households	Persons
Professional, managerial and intermediate non-manual	25·0	20·8	75·0	79·3
Junior non-manual and personal service	57·3	50·2	42·7	49·9
Skilled manual	51·3	49·3	48·7	50·6
Semi-skilled and un-skilled manual	73·5	70·2	26·5	29·8
All classes	50·8	46·9	49·2	53·1

Source: Halvey ed. 1972:551

Welfarism has been a poor palliative. In the United States, for example, the extent of the decline in the numbers of families officially defined as living in poverty has exactly mirrored the growth in national prosperity in the postwar era. The decline in poverty has slowed up commensurately with a falling off in the expansion of incomes and with the growth of unemployment. There can be no mistaking the fact that the state does virtually nothing to protect the disprivileged in hard times, just as it has achieved no redistribution of resources in affluent ones. What is particularly interesting is that organised labour has been only a little more successful in protecting its members than have efforts on behalf of groups lacking the political leverage of industrial action. Average unemployment benefit in the United States in 1960 stood at a figure too low 'to maintain even a single person at a decent standard of living' (Kolko 1962:79). It worked out at around one-third of the weekly average pay, even though it was originally intended that the proportion should be one-half.

The requirements for securing unemployment benefit are stringent, and depend on the recipient's previous record of uninterrupted work. So, those workers who need unemployment benefit most, because of the fluctuating (often seasonal) demand for their services, find it hardest to obtain. In 1957-8, Kolko records, 40 percent of unemployed family heads were receiving no benefit. Discrimination in the matter of income maintenance becomes cumulative as one moves down the class order. Sickness benefits, for example, are also earnings-related. All these forms of welfare are certainly not what Marshall (1950) has called the social rights of citizenship, which he sees as unfolding in conjunction with the civil and political liberties established during the course of the nineteenth century. They are rights stemming from an *employment relationship*, past or present. Most of what ordinarily passes for welfarism is in fact a kind of compulsory savings scheme. Governments spend substantial proportions of their revenue on pensions, school milk, health provision and suchlike, but this should not obscure the fact that, 'much of the redistribution which does take place is of a "horizontal" rather than a "vertical" kind. That is, it is contributions from groups like the young and the unmarried which are largely subsidising payments to the sick or the elderly or those with large families. It is in other words a form of "life cycle" transfer, which does not necessarily entail much movement of resources from one *social* class to another' (Parkin 1972:125).

Titmuss (1965) pushes the argument a good deal further than this. He asserts that the welfare state acts in many ways to enlarge rather than diminish differential life chances. The relative weakness of the state in allocating social advantage has never really been in doubt. In a recession, what is euphemistically known as 'government spending' — public transport, health and education facilities, state housing, pension increases — is always the first thing to be cut. (It is interesting that any growth in these public services is often known as 'government help', a nice comment on the philosophy of welfare.) The thought that the state might actually be channelling resources from the poorer to the better-off, however, has to be taken very seriously. It does not do to accept the idea as an unassailable orthodoxy in a detailed sense. The field of welfare economics is fraught with complexities both of calculation and of what can legitimately be allowed to enter the summation of profit and loss. What is at least unarguable, though, is that it would be wildly awry to confuse the increasing volume of government spending on welfare with the purposive re-allocation of funds on anything but the tiniest scale.

This is all very puzzling, because there are on the statute books in many capitalist countries measures which are unequivocally redistributive in intention, such as estate duty, which provides for punitive rates of taxation on inheritances. The effect of these measures, nevertheless, has been minimal. The principle of the law is that all that is not expressly forbidden is allowed. This is wholly admirable from the point of view of civil and political liberties, but it entails a corresponding weakness on the part of the state in relation to inequalities. Redistributive legislation has not taxed the wealth of the holders so much as their ingenuity. And they have mostly proved quite equal to the occasion. Table 3.1.1 gives one estimate of the changes in the distribution of personal wealth in the United Kingdom during the twentieth century. It would appear that some hefty in-roads have been made into the holdings of the top 1 percent, and in the strict legal sense redistribution has occurred on a fairly large scale. But great scepticism is in order concerning the social reality implied by these figures. Titmuss's *Income Distribution and Social Change* (1962) is a painstaking and superb piece of detective work in track of the missing millions. The basic argument is quite simple, although the ramifications are certainly not. All estimates as to the distribution of income and wealth in Britain are necessarily based on returns to the Income Tax Commissioners. This is a very limiting procedure, because they treat the husband and wife as the unit of accounting and (even more) because any accounting period is necessarily fixed and fairly short — for earned incomes, one year. Two general strategies are therefore open to the very rich. The first is to spread assets round the family, and it is interesting to observe here that in the table the drop in the 1 percent bracket is considerably more dramatic than in the other two rows. The second is to remove assets which come under fire into legally non-taxable forms. The prime instance here is that of death duties, which do not apply if the property is transferred to heirs five years before the death of the donor. Capital gains tax, too, does not apply provided assets are held for a certain period of time before realising a profit. Measures like these do nothing to dissipate the concentration of wealth and economic power.

Two examples will have to suffice for illustration, out of Titmuss's varied catalogue. Within the family, the rich sometimes contract by deed of covenant to support one of its members. In transferring that part of their income they also transfer liability to tax on it. Thus, a covenanter with £10,000 per annum gross unearned income in 1959 who contracted to pay his student son £10 a week while he was at university, involved the taxpayers at large in finding £314.10s a year in lost tax revenue, nothwithstanding that the son was being educated at public expense on a scholarship (Titmuss 1962:84). This example is in fact a hypothetical one, culled from a manual on tax planning. One wide-awake couple, 'living together, with incomes of £5,000 and £1,500 respectively, agreed not to marry, the man then covenanting to pay £1,500 a year to the woman. Subsequently, twins were born and the couple effected a discretionary trust which paid these two children £250 a year each less tax. The couple, who intended to marry when their children were twenty-one, estimated that they would by then have saved £20,000 in tax. This would be settled on the children' (Titmuss 1962:84).

A second well established method of reducing tax liabilities is the formation of a one-man company. By this means the profits of any one year can be registered as those of the company rather than the individual, who then pays himself an annual salary at a rate which does not incur steeply progressive charges such as surtax (Titmuss 1962:118). Another small bonus might, for example, be the running of a 'company' car, the expenses of which are offset against profits. Of course, in some cases, such as that of a small businessman facing an uncertain future, there is both logic and fairness in the arrangement. Still, the general possibilities inherent in such schemes are plain enough. In Britain during the fifties, right against the run in a general decline in small-scale ownership, the number of new private companies tripled, as did the proportion of them with nominal capital of less than £1,000. As the three dissenting members of the Royal Commission on Taxation in 1952 noted, all equity goes by the board in a system which refuses to treat income and wealth in the light of the same general distributive principles.

Because of the operation of a whole array of fiscal devices like these, Titmuss suggests (1965:258), 'the State now makes a larger contribution on average to the pensions of the rich than it does to the pensions of the poor.' It does so, of course, only indirectly, but very effectively, in terms of tax foregone, subsidised private employers' schemes, and so on. Every *private* extension of benefits, in fact, cost the employers next to nothing. The money is found by the generality of taxpayers, and by labour-cost adjustments which (as already pointed out) leave the profits-labour ratio untouched. All forms of hidden income must eventually present themselves as charges on the national budget, and all discriminate to a greater or lesser degree against manual workers, as well as giving a push to inflation which further penalises the lower income groups.

The same tale could be repeated in many areas of state intervention, but one of them is particularly significant from the point of view of class structure — housing. Since the open market remains the overwhelming determinant of the allocation of housing resources, it is no surprise that both the ownership and quality of housing varies markedly between classes. State building and rental programmes, certainly, have inserted a third and increasingly numerous grouping between the owners of domestic property and renters. Rex (1968) has tried to develop a model for the identification of housing classes in urban agglomerations, and though there have been a number of important critiques of that model it is generally agreed that the three basic types of tenure define the parameters within which competition for housing takes place, given the value placed on home ownership in Britain. The three types are readily distinguishable in terms of amenities, security of tenure and (especially) financial advantage. The renters tend to be concentrated in the seedy or shabby-genteel quarters of the city, living in sub-divided elderly houses vacated by the middle classes of an earlier generation in their flight from the urban choke. State housing complexes cater for stable working-class populations. These people, compared to the renters, are in something of a privileged position. They enjoy privacy, good amenities and considerable rights of tenure, and pay out less of the family budget for those things. In terms of amenities, there is nowadays increasing parity between state housing and private ownership. Both government policy and the rising costs of building have pulled from opposite directions to produce a great levelling in this respect. Nevertheless important differences do remain. In the mid-sixties, 60 percent of households 'had a full set of four "standard" domestic facilities for their exclusive use — W.C., bath or shower, basin and hot water', but half of all unskilled and semi-skilled workers' households lacked them (Westergaard and Resler 1975:113-4). In 1966, the number of persons per room was 0.52 in owner-occupied dwellings and 0.70 in local authority properties. In this field too, Titmuss believes, the state subsidises property-owners more generously than those who depend upon it, because of 'the differential effects of local rate payments, housing subsidies, interest rates, tax deductibles for mortgage interest, and other factors' (Titmuss 1965:358). And of course, in the matter of capital gains the private owners score over all other types of occupancy. Generally speaking, owner-occupiers pay little more of their income to achieve the security and profit of freehold rights than other groups do to keep someone else's roof over their head.

But perhaps an even more fundamental consideration is that the housing market creates segregated areas of residence, so that the facts of class inequality are enshrined in bricks and mortar. Speculation in property and the effects of inflation in the booming postwar period have sharpened anxieties and deprivations in the housing market, which has recently started to attract the attention it deserves in the study of inequalities. House-ownership confers a sense of security and a haven against inflation, and those who are shorn of both have become increasingly restive in the big cities. 'Affluence' has meant for many people an intensified battle to keep a decent roof over their heads in the face of monopolistic exploitation and greed. Housing is a sensitive area of social injustice, and one where the claims of private-property rights are perceived with immediacy and understanding. The spread of rent strikes and squatters' movements are rare examples of collective action outside the sphere of production. Urban problems are as often as not class problems at their root, and can only be expected to increase until a greater measure of purposeful control and power passes into the hands of the state planners from private enterprise.

Social Mobility

If the distribution of inequalities has proved remarkably impervious to change, what of social mobility? Classes do not have clear-cut 'boundaries' across which people move with greater or lesser frequency, while leaving the essential character of the class untouched. The prospects of social promotion (or demotion) are an integral part of life chances, and the degree of social closure of the group greatly affects its sense of collective identity.

Career mobility (intragenerational mobility) out of the ranks of the working class is a rare event, at least as far as long-distance movement is concerned. The working and educational experiences which go to make the manual worker are not well suited to the exercise of administrative authority and the social system of the office. Blau and Duncan (1967: 424) report for a very large sample of Americans that the *first* job is decisively correlated with occupational destination at the height of an individual's career. This is exactly what might have been expected, given the growing importance of formal education in job-placement, even though factors peculiar to firms and industries bring about considerable variation in the pattern (Lee 1968). Routine clerical work is not completely closed to manual people, especially if it is closely linked to the shop floor, such as tally-clerking, for instance. Limited promotion on the technical side of management is also more likely than a strictly administrative appointment, but normally the position of foreman is one beyond which even the skilled workers cannot realistically hope to rise — and they know it (Goldthorpe *et al.*, 1968:128-9). Even promotion to foreman is statistically highly improbable, given the ratio of supervisors to operatives in a big firm. In the light of the present discussion, the main point to observe is that this aspect of closure is becoming more, not less, pronounced.

> 'For those who leave non-selective secondary schools at the age of fifteen for a manual occupation, this kind of work is becoming more than ever before a life sentence. The same factors that are making for more intergenerational mobility — technological progress, increasing specialisation and the growing importance of education in occupational placement — are also operating to reduce the possibility of "working up from the bottom" in industry, and are thus indirectly re-emphasising the staff-worker dichotomy' (Goldthorpe and Lockwood 1963:80).

Rates of intergenerational mobility are considerably higher for a complex of reasons. Something like a quarter to a third of manual workers' children move into middle-class occupations, while the social elevator carries about the same proportion of non-manual workers' offspring in the opposite direction. However, these figures conceal the very modest distance travelled. Most of the movement takes place within what Parkin has christened the 'buffer zone' of skilled manual and lower white-collar occupations. Long-range mobility in either direction is rare indeed. Above all, in no case do middle-class children enjoy an advantage of less than 2.5:1 over manual progeny in their chances of obtaining middle-class employment for themselves (Miller 1969: *passim*). The picture overall, therefore, is one of considerable impermeability of the class frontiers, which is closely connected with the ability of the middle classes to protect their children from social descent.

Sociologists remain heavily indebted to the comparative

studies of mobility carried out by Lipset and Bendix (1959). They rightly stress that not 'measurement but the investigation of causes and effects, is the object of research into social mobility'. In one critical respect, however, they ignored their own methodological recommendations, by in fact treating the analysis of rates of mobility in isolation from the consideration of the social mechanisms which might explain them. This approach led to some unexpected and baffling conclusions. Reviewing their own empirical material, Lipset and Bendix observe (1959:13) that

> '*The overall pattern of social mobility appears to be much the same in the industrial societies of various Western countries*. This is startling. . . . Further, although it is clear that social mobility is related in many ways to the economic expansion of industrial societies, it is at least doubtful that the rates of mobility and of expansion are correlated. Since a number of the countries for which we have data have had different rates of economic expansion but show comparable rates of mobility, our tentative interpretation is that the social mobility of societies becomes relatively high once their industrialisation, and hence their economic expansion, reaches a certain level'.

Here is how their findings look in tabular form:

Table 3.5.1 Comparative indices of upward and downward mobility (%)

Country	Upward mobility (Non-manual sons of manual fathers)	Downward mobility (Manual sons of non-manual fathers)	Total vertical mobility
United States	33	26	30
Germany	29	32	31
Sweden	31	24	29
Japan	36	22	27
France	39	20	27
Switzerland	45	13	23

Source: Lipset and Bendix 1959:25, table 2.1 (adapted).

With hindsight, it is easy to see what is wrong with this conclusion. Lipset and Bendix have taken up a position (though a tentative one) which is indistinguishable from a functionalist argument. That is to say, mobility is seen as deriving from systemic processes, as 'economic development' 'causes' changes in the rates of mobility. If the facts of mobility, on the other hand, are tied closely to the explanation of *how* changes between positions are effected, then a very different picture emerges. This is the burden of Miller's (1969) essay. As a result, we now treat the economic system as only one variable in mobility rates. Certainly, rapid economic expansion has the effects of creating more white-collar and skilled manual jobs. Both farm people and unskilled workers have, therefore, considerable chances for upward mobility, without anyone being compelled to move downwards to make room for them. This is often referred to as *structural* (or structurally induced) mobility, caused by a change in the distribution of occupations themselves. But of at least equal interest are the social mechanisms which work to pattern mobility under conditions of competition for high-status jobs. So, Miller suggests, one should give a great deal of attention to patterns of downward mobility. The shifts down the class order are likely to be revealing in that they will indicate the extent to which those favourably placed in the class hierarchy are able to protect their children from social descent. It is particularly the *openness* or otherwise of societies which has been of central concern both to sociologists and ideologues. Miller constructed a rough index of openness, by recording the rate of movement from manual into non-manual occupations intergenerationally, and setting it against the rate of self-recruitment within the non-manual stratum.

Technically simple as it is, this device shows up some quite important variations in the patterns of mobility in capitalist societies, which are concealed in the first table. The fact is that the concept of 'total vertical mobility' is not sociologically all that helpful. Given Miller's operation upon the figures, it can be seen (by way of example) that the children of manual workers in Belgium have the best chances of rising into middle-class occupations. At the same time, it remains a

Table 3.5.2 Social self-recruitment and upward mobility

Country	(1) Non-manual into non-manual %	(2) Manual into non-manual %	(3) Index of openness (1 over 2) %
Great Britain	57.9	24.8	234
Denmark	63.2	24.1	262
U.S.A.	77.4	28.7	270
Sweden	72.3	25.5	284
Norway	71.4	23.2	308
France	79.5	30.1	264
Netherlands	56.8	19.6	290
Belgium	96.6	30.9	313
West Germany	71.0	20.0	355
Italy	63.5	8.5	747

Source: Miller 1969:330, table 3 (adapted).

relatively 'closed' class order, because this upward mobility has not been at the expense of non-manual children, 96.6 percent of whom moved into similar occupations. Virtually all mobility in that country has been of the upward, structural variety. To speak of a closed class system in Miller's terminology, incidentally, does not allow direct inferences about the degree of class conflict and class consciousness in them. The index of openness is a purely objective measure of the *rate of exchange* between occupational positions. A high index of openness could well indicate considerable class tensions stemming from the competition for high-status positions, whereas a high rate of structural mobility yields a situation where large segments of the population can either make upward gains or stay where they are. And of course, intergenerational mobility is only one possible causal factor in class consciousness. But all this does mean, certainly, that the formulation of Lipset and Bendix needs emendation. Instead of saying, as they do, that the overall *pattern* of social mobility is similar for most industrial countries, it is more accurate to say that the overall *rates* of mobility are very similar. The term 'pattern' then can be reserved for referring to the factors underlying mobility rates, such as the part played by structural mobility in creating them, the ratio of downward to upward mobility, and so on.

Education is increasingly and overwhelmingly the means by which occupational success is achieved, though this is not to say that it is by itself sufficient to predict occupational destination. Formal credentials could be better likened to the ticket you need in order to play bingo — no ticket, no prize. And it is well understood that educational contests are the prime means by which the working class is denied social mobility. Predictably the middle-class outlook finds concentrated expression and reward in attitudes to education. It would be otiose to enumerate the myriad factors which influence *individual* performance in the educational system, such as position among siblings, size of the family, work experience of the mother, and so on. The main point is that middle-class children win scholastic preferment with a regularity which shows that these various influences do not typically pull in different directions. Class barriers restrict social exchanges with persons who might provide greater stimulus and ambition to the working-class child. Educationalists themselves may well reinforce the influences of parents and peers, because class is the basis of discriminatory expectations (Kerckhoff 1972:127). Even where some degree of social mix is achieved within the school, streaming is a means by which class differences reassert themselves (Ford 1969). Working-class children do break out of the vicious circle, but at the cost of much greater social and intellectual struggles than their middle-class peers. Sewell *et al.* (1957:72) show for the United States that of the most gifted male high-school students in their sample (with an I.Q. level of 119 +), 66 percent had high-level educational aspirations in the lowest socio-economic group. This was exactly the same proportion as the students from the highest socio-economic group with an I.Q. level of 102-9. Only a quarter of the students in this intelligence bracket from the most deprived homes had similar ambitions for continuing their education. This brings home the very important point that it is among the average performers, whose academic future teeters in the balance, that parental influences are the most critical. Jackson and Marsden (1963) demonstrate what a contribution can be made to educational attainment by parents with the tenacity and resource to pursue their objectives in defiance of the judgment of the schools. It can be done only by an insistence that the educational system can and should be made to serve their purposes, and by a refusal to be cowed by authority. These middle-class parents and their children showed a grinding and instrumental approach to education, but there can be no question of the efficiency with which they used the schooling system.

The disabilities suffered by working-class children in educational competition have been partially relieved by the expansion of opportunities. Little and Westergaard (1964: 309, table 4) show for Britain that the expansion of higher education has indeed been of advantage to the working class, but the absolute numbers of middle-class children similarly graced has been very large, so that inequality in this field remains very striking. Of higher professionals' children born before 1910, 37 percent found their way into universities, as opposed to 1 percent of unskilled and semi-skilled workers' offspring. Among the cohorts born in the late 1930s these proportions were 62 percent and 10 percent. The figures indicate something considerably less than a transformation, particularly in view of the postwar institution of financial aid for higher study. Any final judgment about the effect of change on the structure of working-class opportunity must, in fairness, be held in abeyance. Reforms took place mostly during the early fifties, and it will be some time yet before fuller information is available about the career paths of those who grew up under the new dispensations. What evidence there is suggests a slight and continuing improvement in the chances of working-class children, while non-manual families have nonetheless successfully staked a claim to a lion's share of the new opportunities created (Westergaard and Resler 1975:323).

Still hanging over the discussion, however, is the question of how far increasing equality of educational opportunity can be translated into *market* advantages. France is a better case for study in this context, because its student numbers are relatively high, and the problem of graduate employment has been fairly pressing for a number of years past. Marceau's findings are very interesting in that she is able to identify a trend which may easily be concealed by the bare statistics on representation. There is a process of selection going on not only between the levels of the French educational system, but within them too. Thus, working-class graduates usually come from those faculties with the worst chances on the labour market. Even at the bottom of the pyramid of learning, this pecking order is repeated. The technical schools cater for the academic duds, channelling their pupils into jobs as foremen and supervisors in industry. Yet only the children of skilled workers get anything like parity of access to places in them. In these school as well 'the academic and social hierarchies are apparent: the students of electrical trades and mechanics are, for instance, from higher social backgrounds than their colleagues in the boiler-making or the building trades. . . . Pupils coming from the lycees and comprehensives, the "failures" of the secondary schools, are oriented to the better trades, and never to the building ones for example' (Marceau 1974:219). The question of elite education apart, therefore, working-class children find it difficult to *compete* with the middle classes, so that any occupational mobility they may experience will depend very heavily on demographic and structural features of the occupational order. This might have been predicted from the earlier discussion, of course, but it is essential to get the distinction between social mobility and educational opportunity firmly established.

Once the difference is made clear, a further set of objections to end-of-ideologism presents itself. The effects on class structure of any liberalisation of educational opportunity are highly ambiguous under some circumstances. Whatever parents and pupils feel about the intrinsic rewards of study, they quite definitely expect it to have a market value too. But will the occupational structure provide commensurate opportunities? It is part of the end-of-ideologist faith that it

Table 3.6 Indices of growth of main occupational groups in Britain 1911-59

Occupational group	'000s in 1911	1959 figure as % of 1911
1A. Higher professionals	184	297
1B. Lower professionals	560	238
2A. Employers and proprietors (a)	1,232	99*
2B. Managers and administrators	608	200*
3. Clerical workers	887	327
4. Foremen, inspectors, supervisors	236	272
5. Skilled workers	5,608	106
6. Semi-skilled workers	7,244	104
7. Unskilled workers	1,767	159

(a) this group might be better labelled 'petty bourgeoisie'. There would be very few large-scale employers among them by 1951. In that year over 60% of them were one-man businesses.
* this figure refers to the 1951:1911 ratio.
Source: Routh 1965:7, table 2, (adapted).

will. The accompanying table shows that the main areas of white-collar growth have been in clerical work and in the lower professions. In percentage terms, the jobs carrying the highest rewards have expanded rapidly, but from a very narrow base, so that their absolute numbers remain small. The table, while it refers to Britain, would apply equally well to any other capitalist country. The United States, it is true, has about half its workforce employed in non-manual jobs, but the area of expansion is the same — in the more menial occupations. In other countries, manual workers make up about three-quarters of the workforce, and there is very little sign of anything but the most marginal changes during recent decades (Giddens 1973:178). To some extent the impression of mobility may do service for the actuality, but this is most unlikely to remain true if diploma-inflation not true mobility becomes the experience of working-class children generally.

Far from having a 'safety-valve' effect, extended education could raise expectations which are frustrated in the labour market, a situation which Parkin (1972:65) suggests may help to explain high rates of youthful deviance in the United States.

A general point needs to be made here. While a mass of studies have dealt with problems relating to the individual within the educational system, little has been done to show how any given system of education is articulated with the distribution of power and privilege. It is often casually assumed that educational change, like mobility, reflects the 'needs' of the modern industrial order, though in fact a case for such a functional adaptation is very hard to defend. Working-class student representation in universities is certainly not amenable to this kind of explanation, since in the European states there is a definite inverse relationship between it and industrial power. Political factors seem a better guide in this instance. Social-democratic governments in Norway and Sweden presided after the war over the dismantling of the selective schooling system, with a consequently rapid rise in the numbers of workers' children entering universities (Parkin 1972:113). However, just to remind us that sociological explanations are never that simple, there is the peculiar case of the U.K. It has a notoriously elitist educational system, yet the highest proportion of manual workers' offspring in higher education. Nor can this be attributed to the flush of postwar egalitarianism initiated by the 1944 Education Act. Extraordinarily enough, the percentage of working-class students in British universities has remained static at least since 1928, when they made up 23 percent of the student body, (Halsey ed., 1972:191). Although the political colouration of governments may be of some relevance, therefore, any comparative figures have to be regarded with some care.

The British university system is very much an oddity. The chief reason for its success in operating a high degree of academic meritocratism is the haphazard and decentralised growth of the higher education sector, quite out of keeping with the type of bureaucratic university that governments imposed, for example, in France and Germany, with their far

Table 3.7 Percentage of university students of working-class origin in European countries circa 1960

	%		%
Great Britain	25	France	8
Norway	25	Austria	8
Sweden	16	Netherlands	5
Denmark	10	West Germany	5

Source: Parkin 1972:110

stronger traditions of *etatisme*. As a result the system itself is stratified to an extent not found elsewhere, and it is not the possession of a degree but its provenance which has to be considered. The British working-class student representation is put into a sharper perspective by the fact that at Oxford and Cambridge they form 13 percent of the total — half the overall proportion, and a figure much closer to those for the other European countries. And it is from Oxbridge, plus, to a lesser degree from London and the Scottish foundations that most recruitment into the economic and administrative bureaucracies of corporate capitalism takes place. Britain, however, is only unique insofar as it combines its elite educational institutions with a small number of students overall, which tends to accentuate the exclusiveness of the university system. The Ivy League colleges evidently play a similar role in the very open educational organisation of the United States, and the remarks of a dean of admissions at Harvard makes it clear that there, too, the barriers to working-class mobility are as much social as intellectual. With disarming condescension, he made the point that scholarship assistance to the needy applicant would only be granted if the student were both personally and academically outstanding. If he were merely 'very good' then the policy would be to reward him with a certificate of admission, but no money, leaving him to attend a local, less prestigious institution and to leave attendance at Harvard to his son (quoted by Kolko 1962:70).

Table 3.8 Graduates of working-class origin in different university groups

University group	*Percentage of working-class origin* *Men*	*Women*
Oxbridge	13	6
London	24	18
Scottish	24	20
Smaller Civic	30	22
Larger Civic	35	23
Wales	43	34
ALL UNIVERSITIES	26	20
No.	2422	717

Source: Kelsall *et. al.,* 1972:191

Of course, no account of elite education in Britain could pass over the strong links between the ancient universities and the public schools, which appear to function as even more critical 'selectors' for recruitment to elite positions. That is, although higher education is a prerequisite for many such positions, it is typically an Oxbridge higher education, access to which is heavily influenced in turn by public school origins. That is, Oxbridge is a kind of finishing school for a tiny segment of the secondary level, while it is also a ground for the recruitment and socialisation of able children from more varied milieux. In general, however, the attendance at a public school continues to be the more decisive experience for inclusion among 'top people' in Britain, especially attendance at one of the half-dozen most exclusive of them. These schools, which as Martin and Crouch point out, 'contain less than 3 percent of all boys aged fourteen, and 16.5 per cent of all boys in sixth forms', provided the following proportions of incumbents to elite positions (see table 3-9).

What has been achieved in Britain, then, is a fairly high degree of *academic* meritocracy, which was granted readily and early because academic success and class privilege are only loosely linked within the system as a whole. Different

Table 3.9 Percentage of posts filled by those with a public school education in Britain in the fifties and sixties

Conservative Cabinet (1964)	87
Judges	76
Conservative M.P.s	76
Ambassadors (1953)	70
Lieutenants-General and above (1953)	70
Governors of the Bank of England (1958)*	67
Chief Executives, 100 largest companies (1963)	64
Civil Servants, above Assistant Secretary (1950)	59
Directors of leading firms (1956)	58
All City Directors*	47
Labour Cabinet (1964)	35
Labour M.P.s (1964)	15

* Only six of the leading schools

Source: Martin and Crouch 1971:255, table 8, (adapted).

universities, and hence different sectors of the secondary system and different class 'mixes', still operate to feed very distinctive parts of the occupational order. Class of degree and subject do influence occupational choice in some measure, but social class influences remain very strong. Working-class students (and students from 'working-class' universities) still tend to move into teaching, research and design in industry, or into university teaching. The civil service, management and the more exclusive professions remain the prime stamping ground of middle-class students, particularly those with a public school and/or Oxbridge background (Kelsall *et al.*, 1972:ch.2). To some extent, the occupational preferences of working-class students would seem to reflect a lack of familiarity with the alternatives, a certain restriction of social vision generated by their origins. A similar finding was made by Timperley and Gregory (1971) among secondary school children, fully four-fifths of whom had no real informed basis for choice, and simply divided up the occupational structure into 'education' and 'commerce' as representing their range of options. Knowledge of the more glamorous and unusual jobs was conspicuously absent, as was an understanding of the strategies required to attain them. In addition, however, it is clear enough that employers discriminate against working-class graduates, though whether this is a deliberate matter or not is open to debate. In any event, it is indisputable that the social setting of the university itself is not a melting-pot of the classes. Class cleavages continue to operate in the patterning of friendships, and in some ways the relatively greater number of working-class children in universities, as opposed to the upper forms of the schools, reinforces established class differences by providing a sub-culture in which the upwardly mobile can collectively resist the middle-class norms which the institution fosters. All these points are made by Kelsall and his colleagues, and it is worthwhile repeating their overall judgment on the relationship between university education and work. They state that,

> 'here we have observed the importance of social differentiation even between those who are ostensibly academic equals in the highest-ranking sector of education in our society. For the university graduates in this study clearly did not have equal opportunities in the world of work, even if they experienced an identical form of education and had performed equally well or badly. They were (apart from their qualifications) not part of a common culture, but had come up to university with attitudes profoundly influenced by their family backgrounds and these were in many cases reinforced and certainly not attenuated by the process of higher education itself. And when they came to seek employment in the particularly high-status sections, social class influences were reinforced by the images and preferences of prospective employers themselves' (Kelsall *et al.*, 1972:99).

From the point of view of class theory, all this makes plain, any question about the distribution of educational opportunity must be of the form 'education for what?'. Although the British university system is quirkily egalitarian in one sense, in another it is wholly typical of its continental European counter-parts. In France, for example, exactly the same role of social selector is played by the *Grandes Ecoles* in weeding out working-class academic fliers as is performed by the Oxbridge system. Only 4 percent of working-class children find their way into these 'super-universities', which train their students for posts in the highest echelons of the administration of the state and economy. Industry, government and the civil service is dominated by these graduates. The *Grandes Ecoles* are centres of academic excellence, but it is a distinct social type which they are bent on creating. The fact that elite educational institutions in Britain are found equally at the secondary as at the tertiary level underlines the sociological principle at work, which is that educational attainment is more of a legitimating symbol than a matter of qualifications. If they studied Assyrian it would not matter — indeed, the British system continues to be heavily biased in favour of humanistic training for its civil service. The desired end product is the 'gentleman' or 'jeune monsieur' in both instances. As the head of one *Grande Ecole* put it,

> 'You must learn the social milieu of the "senior executives" of the nation, which you are going to join if you are not already there. Do not neglect any aspect of its usages *savoir-faire*. I even dare to add, hurry and acquaint yourself with this milieu before you choose your wife. . . . for you will both suffer if she should be ill at ease and not do you justice' (quoted by Marceau 1974:229-30).

Even graduation by no means marks the end of this process of watchful socialisation within the corridors of power. Within the Civil Service in both France and Britain there is an unmistakeable hierarchy, with the Treasury at the top. Here too social class influences are found at work. In France, higher officials in the 'social' ministries, such as Health and Education, come from working-class backgrounds in about 14 percent of cases. The nearer one moves towards the elite corps within the service, the fewer such officials are: to take the two extreme examples, in the Treasury 5.5 percent, and in the Prime Minister's secretariat a mere 2 percent (Marceau 1974:226). Notwithstanding the intense filtering provided by the formal educational process, that is, there is a further set a mechanisms which distance those of working-class origin from the government departments carrying most power and prestige.

Capitalism and Elite Theory

These, then, are some of the salient facts concerning inequalities in 'modern, industrial' societies, and they do not square at all well with the basic assumptions – either theoretical or empirical – on which end-of-ideologists rest their case. All the weaknesses in end-of-ideologism can be finally tracked down to its failure to cope adequately with the problem of power in relation to elite formation. Very often, the deficiency consists in simply brushing the whole question under the carpet. *Political Man*, for example, contains within its 400-odd pages only four brief references to 'power' and 'the state', three of which occur in the context of a discussion of Marx. This neglect is itself a reflection of the fact that 'power', as Weber, for example, understood the term, is defined out of existence. Bell (1962:45) has put his case on this issue as follows:

> 'Two "silent" revolutions in the relations between power and class position in modern society seem to be in process. One is a change in the *mode of access* to power insofar as inheritance alone is no longer all-determining; the other is a change in the *nature of power-holding itself* insofar as technical skill rather than property, and political position rather than wealth, have become the basis on which power is wielded.'

Considered as hypotheses, these are interesting and important statements, but they do very little to advance our understanding of observed social processes. They do not tell us what kind of technical skill is required to inherit and pass on massive property advantages; nor why the technical skill necessary for elite positions which cannot be transmitted through bequest should be the monopoly of privileged strata. These are omissions common to all functionalist accounts of stratification and power, to which end-of-ideologism owes its theoretical inspiration. (See Davis and Moore 1945; Davis 1948:ch. 14; Parsons 1966; and for their critics, Buckley 1958; Huaco 1966; Giddens 1968.) Least of all is it clear, if private-property interests have been subordinated to the general will of the political community, why extremes of wealth and poverty should continue to flourish? As another close student of democracy has remarked, there seems to be something inherently wrong in the argument that the people are both sovereign and poor.

Preferences for politically deodorised labels such as 'industrial' and 'post-capitalist' society do not alter the fact that economic power is still massively concentrated in a few hands, and backed by the forces of the law and a dominant public ethos. There is no objection to being ideologically *parti pris*, to arguing, as Lipset does (1963:403), that democracy is the good society in action. What is at stake here is a scientific principle, not an ideological one. To lose sight of the fact that the social democracies are capitalist societies is to abandon the chief clue to everyday social processes in them:

> 'There *is* a profit motive at the heart of industry, industrial relations *are* based on collective bargaining, there *are* political parties representing "both sides of industry", the Conservative Party, backed by at least some industrialists, *has* in recent years sought to invoke the law against trade unions, the police and the military do *not* show signs of disaffection, and Bishops, Judges, Vice-Chancellors and media pundits *do* continually work to sustain a morality which is at least not inimical to the needs of capitalism' (Rex 1974:214).

This does not mean that there may not have been an important period of decline in the intensity of class conflict in the postwar world. But it is no *explanation* to say that 'Greater economic productivity is associated with a more equitable distribution of consumption goods and education — factors contributing to a reduction of intra-societal tension' (Lipset 1975:214).
This is nothing more than technological determinism appeal-

ing to a non-existent set of facts. Technology creates greater wealth, but its distribution is a political matter. Every improvement in the condition of the disprivileged in capitalist societies has been conditional upon gains for all. Poverty and unemployment, and inferior housing and health care, are widespread and increasing. In a society in which full employment and rising standards of living are proclaimed as a right which governments are bound to support, the possibilities for class conflict are, on the contrary, immense.

With the onset of recession around 1970, these possibilities have been realised in the renewal of large-scale, protracted strikes and the increasing political intervention by governments in industrial relations. This fact draws attention to two further central features of end-of-ideologism. One is the drastic foreshortening of historical perspective entailed by taking the postwar 'boom' years — which lasted for less than a generation — as evidence for a total transformation of the capitalist economies. It is tacitly assumed that the conditions for free collective bargaining are an eternal fact of life, which they are obviously not. This view is closely related to the second strand of end-of-ideologist thinking, which is that economic management presents a set of purely technical problems for which solutions lie ready to hand. The term 'capitalist' can be avoided, because 'industrialism' is conceived of as a sort of self-equilibrating system presided over by experts. Here, the influence of a bowdlerised Weberianism is detectable. Weber emphasised the possibility of a controlled, sustained growth by capitalism in which technical and bureaucratic expertise were indispensable. He continued, however, to speak of *capitalism*; and it is worth mentioning that he actually viewed the concentration of economic control as a potential source of the crises of capitalism (Weber 1968:128-9), originating in the conflict between short- and long-term economic rationality. And he certainly did not equate 'functional indispensability' with power over decision-making, remarking that slaves are indispensable in certain types of society. Insofar as end-of-ideologists speak of 'power' at all (which is extremely rarely) they use it in the emasculated sense of 'expertise'; and then, very puzzlingly, locate it in the middle-class specialists leaving only speculation about what they are in the middle of. This feat of levitation is, however, an illusion, since specialists operate within a framework of policy which they administer but certainly do not determine.

The plausibility of the illusion is heightened by the complexity of the connections between propertied interests and the state, in contrast to the days when lack of property was itself a political disqualification. The scope and range of state activity have so far enlarged as to be beyond the controlling capacities of a private political club. There has occurred a corresponding transformation of what Giddens (1973:121) calls the 'mediation of control', which he very usefully contrasts with the 'institutional mediation of power':

> 'By the institutional mediation of power, I mean the general form of state and economy within which elite groups are recruited and structured. This concerns, among other things, the role of property in the overall organisation of economic life, the nature of the legal framework defining economic and political rights and obligations, and the institutional structure of the state itself. The mediation of control refers to the actual (effective) power of policy-formation and decision-making held by the members of particular elite groups: how far, for example, economic leaders are able to influence decisions taken by politicians, etc.'

The theory of the so-called 'managerial revolution' is one persistent form taken by exaggerated claims concerning the significance of the 'rise of the middle classes'. This theory has, in fact, appeared in two diametrically opposed forms, both of which see a fundamental change stemming from the separation between ownership and control of the means of production. According to Burnham (1962), this change consists in the rise of a new ruling class based on *de facto* power over the economy. In its end-of-ideologist version, the managerial revolution means the end of the mad, bad days of entrepreneurial rapacity, and of the industrial and social unrest which it brought in its train. The modern manager, it is argued, lacks the means of compulsion conferred by the ownership of property. He is therefore obliged to manage his workforce by negotiation and consensus (Dahrendorf 1959:45). Furthermore, the professional manager is a career man, not a buccaneer. His interests lie in the stable, long-term growth of the company he represents. As such, he will prefer optimal expansion to the quick but de-stabilising forays into the market characteristic of the owner-entrepreneur. The managerial stratum is thus held to have interposed itself between the conflicting interests of capital and labour, to the benefit of society as a whole.

The striking changes in the organisation and functioning of corporate capitalism, Westergaard and Resler observe (1975:156), do not in themselves contain an answer to the real question at issue, which is how businesses *act*. Since both governments and business spokesmen insist that a profitable and competitive private economic sector is the basis of social well-being, it is hard to believe that the profit motive has ceased to be the guiding force of business operations. Claims concerning the moral transformation in business attitudes as a result of managerial control must always run up against the uncomfortable argument that

> 'managers still operate in a capitalist market and hence must be just as oriented to the traditional capitalist goal, profit, as owners. This argument was completely confirmed by our observations .... The indicators of successful performance are profits, growth, and return on investment. The essence of the professional manager is his rigorous and exclusive dedication to financial values. He represents a return to the values of hard, unameliorated, unconstrained capitalism' (Pahl and Winkler 1974:118).

The rationalisation of capitalist productive techniques, in fact, and their integration through the use of the political apparatus of the state, has been designed precisely to enhance the possibility of consistent economic performance. These changes were not intended to make economic elites more socially accountable, and there is no evidence that managers see their role in that light.

It is true that professional managers have a quite distinct sense of social identity in relation to owners, whom they appear often to regard as misguided, gentlemanly bumblers in a hard world (Pahl and Winkler 1974:119). Far from having basic divergences of interest, however, professional managers are commonly brought in to family firms to rescue them from the depredations of amateurism. This permanent coalition of interests is expressed in two ways. On the one hand, the relationship between managers and controllers of capital is based on a reciprocal dependence, since (as table 3.1.2 shows) managers do *not* typically confront a large number of small shareholders. Control is highly centralised — not necessarily in individual or family hands, but through the operation of banks and other financial consortia as well. Furthermore, the rewards of success in the world of top-level management themselves blur the social significance of the distinction between ownership and control. Although the personal wealth of managers is tiny in relation to the aggregate total of capital, one British survey of directors showed them to be 'by far the wealthiest of the various elite and professional groups covered' (Westergaard and Resler 1975:161). The sums paid to the masters of the giant economic bureaucracies in the form of salaries, expenses and preferential stock issues make it ludicrous to conceive of them as in any sense 'middle class'. Nor can their functions be said in any usual sense of the word to involve technical expertise. The larger the company, the less time its board will spend on matters concerned with the internal running of the firm, and the more its directors must become essentially *political* animals, looking to the overall financial management of the enterprise, negotiating with government, keeping an eye on national and international competition, and suchlike (Brown 1973:94-5). In view of this, it is not very startling to discover (table 3.9) that the social backgrounds of the managers of the giant companies are indistinguishable from those of other elite groups. Furthermore, control is becoming more, not less, concentrated, with the trend toward oligopoly based on a small number of national and multi-national empires. There is much here, in fact, to support Mills' assertion (1956:147) that there has occurred 'the managerial reorganisation of the propertied classes into the more or less unified stratum of the corporate rich'. Stated in a negative and more conservative fashion, there is at least no evidence that the rise of new managerial-cum-administrative elites within corporate capitalism is incompatible with class domination based on private property and the market.

The justification for such distinctions is their explanatory value, and the role of the state in contemporary capitalism highlights the continuities in the institutional mediation of power. Despite increased nationalisation and commitment to welfare policies, the impact of state activity on the structure of inequalities is minimal. Aid to private enterprise is doled out in millions, while public servants are expected, as part of their duties, to track down women who are state beneficiaries and suspected of 'cohabiting'. The administrative agencies of the state are used to relieve the worst human casualties of the system, but this has been true since Poor Law days. Ideologically, Piven and Cloward argue (1974:3) welfarism is dominated by the Poor Law mentality — not among those who administer the system, but in political intention, which is to demean the recipients and to make even the most futile and poorly-paid work seem desirable by comparison. The protection of the old, the sick and the unemployed is carried out in the most niggardly fashion, and the 'citizenship rights' which the state confers in the field of social welfare little more than the fulfillment of a labour contract. The social rights of private wealth, as many have pointed out, are not conditional upon any such evidence of industriousness. Elite education shows how class privilege breaks down the boundaries of the separate institutional orders within the state to link the army, civil service and government offices with private property and the economic bureaucracies of capitalism. Elite education does not by itself guarantee the stability of the capitalist state, but it helps. Its function as a 'selector' in elite mobility brings together into command roles people who share a common cast of mind while excluding those who do not conform to the required social pattern. And all this is completely compatible with the most stringent application of the rules of formal meritocracy, because the chance to succeed is rigged from the outset.

Notice that the choice between those who claim that capitalist elites constitute (on one level) a unified status group, and the sort of theory proposed by Bell, is a choice between an admittedly speculative and incomplete explanation of the facts and *no explanation at all*. There is, however, a second line of defence available. Leaving aside the awkward questions raised by patterns of elite recruitment, it is still possible to claim that those who occupy the command roles in society have no common purpose or basis for action which would entitle us to use terms like 'ruling class' or 'power elite' (Bell 1962:ch.3). Bell's target here — as so often among writers of the end-of-ideologist persuasion — is C. Wright Mills' book *The Power Elite*. Essentially, Bell objects to the picture of purposeful, conspiratorial manipulation of the masses by the power elite which he finds in Mills. In particular, Bell rejects Mills' preoccupation with discussions of 'power' rather than decision-making, and complains of the tendency of *The Power Elite* to gloss over the plain evidence of elite conflict. For example,

> 'Except in a vague, ideological sense, there are relatively few issues on which the managerial elite is united' (Bell 1962:63).

Now, whether or not Mills is guilty of exaggerating the conspiratorial aspect of the exercise of power in American society — itself a debatable point — is not a matter of great importance. The fact is that Mills deliberately set out to examine, not open, democratic decision-making, but the means by which elites could circumscribe the limits within which decision-making took place. Furthermore, the 'vague, ideological' consensus among elites is a matter of critical importance. All social differentiation is a relative matter, and divisions of class interests are quite compatible with an overriding unity of purpose. All Bell has succeeded in expressing is the truism that elite cohesion is always a matter of broad agreement on the basic principles of social organisation and strategies for political action, which cannot in the nature of things preclude economic competition in a capitalist system.

As Bell himself observes, the 'problem of *who unites with whom on what* is an empirical question', but it is not a problem which can be resolved by the inspection of decision-making processes. It also involves teasing out the assumptions which elite figures take for granted, and which thus serve as guiding principles in the exercise of *institutionalised* power, which is what Weber meant by 'domination'. To say that elite groups compete for influence using the democratic processes of political mobilisation is not enough (see Lukes 1975: *passim* for a useful overview of the problems raised only superficially here). It is also essential, as Mills was concerned to point out, to know the range of issues over which they compete, and (by extension) to pinpoint the boundaries within which elite conflict typically occurs. The case of the judiciaries in the western democracies is a good one for illustrating the general argument. It is nonsense to say that the legal profession as a whole has been the compliant tool of capitalist interests, if by this is meant that the law is nothing more than the punitive arm of the state. On the contrary, lawyers have in a real and important sense been independent of political influences, and have done much to preserve civil and political liberties. It still remains true, argues Miliband (1969:143), that the relations between trade unions and the law has been one of 'an unending struggle against the courts' attempts to curb and erode the unions' ability to defend their members' interests'. This conservatism, furthermore, runs far beyond the necessities imposed by statutes. Judges are not mouthpieces of the law; they make it, within the wide limits set by parliamentary legislation, through their interpretations and judgments. That the law operates to favour some interests at the expense of others is just as much an 'empirical question' as any study of decision-making, however exhaustive. And to ask why this is so brings us back to those other questions which end-of-ideologism resolutely ignores: why the judiciary recruits from a strikingly narrow class base, and how the interests of lawyers as a group are bound up with those of private property.

Again, although there might be legitimate reservations about the degree to which social interaction is the basis (and expression) of elite solidarity, as Mills argues, it is hardly probable that it has no relevance to an understanding of how power is wielded. The work of Lupton and Wilson (1973) has uncovered a highly ramified kinship network linking top decision-makers in Britain; in particular the close connections between 'economic' and 'political' personnel. When a social group is found to be characterised by intermarriage and by shared experiences of elite education, it requires a specially trained scepticism to maintain that the members are fundamentally divided against each other. Another useful indication of the homogeneity of a group is the extent to which circulation between elite positions is possible. Here, the close connections between business and conservative political parties clamours to be explained, if Bell's theory of elite recruitment has any validity. But the notion of elite circulation also, as Miliband points out (1969:123 ff.), raises questions about the 'neutrality' of top civil servants, who are traditionally supposed to be above party politics in their professional capacity. Yet as the institutional lines between 'state' and 'economy' have become increasingly blurred, movement between the civil service and private industry has become an entirely normal matter. This hardly suggests any tension between the ethics of business and those of the dedicated state servant. And it is just as well to remember that the recruitment of top-level state servants is also controlled by the even simpler process of political screening (Miliband 1969: 124), making it unlikely that the civil servant's neutrality could ever be severely tested.

In a way, all this states what is obvious. But this is just what end-of-ideologism forces us to do, by propounding a 'commonsense' view of society; a view in which, because class rule is served in any obvious coercive way, no group has power to shape the life of society at the expense of another. (This possibility is apparently limited to one-party states.) To argue otherwise, as many critics have pointed out, does not commit the sociologist to maintaining that capitalist societies are ruled by informal cliques — as in the 'country-house weekend' theory which from time to time surfaces as an explanation of how the ruling class in Britain has concerted its policy on the grouse moors. In a very real sense, Anderson observes, capitalist societies are *not* 'ruled', but in a sense quite different from that entailed by a balance of power between the classes:

> 'How many businessmen resolutely decide that they must leave schools and hospitals to rot, and press on with doubling their TV commercials and lacquering their reception rooms with the money saved? Do any at all? . . . These decisions are not taken in the board room or the bank manager's suite or even the exclusive club or the pleasure yacht. They are taken *nowhere*. They are *not taken*, they are not decisions: fatalities. Nobody calculates and enacts them, they happen unmeant. Our callous and malformed priorities are the prodigious obverse of a thousand discrete, blameless gestures' (quoted by Blackburn 1965:118).

In the same way, the servants of the state (Miliband's phrase) are not drawn further into a plot with each step nearer the positions of authority in society. Patterns of elite recruitment are not necessarily the outcome of a conscious process of selection. As in the case of senior civil servants, objective criteria of 'expertise' will have the same excluding effect. But this expertise is not a fund of technical knowledge: it is expertise in administering a *particular* form of state and society (Miliband 1969:123). Thus the capitalist bureaucracies – private and public alike – become the means by which a continuous process of co-optation of new elite members is carried out. The professional ideal of the civil servant is in fact a kind of practising end-of-ideologist; the administrator *sine ira ac studio*, as Weber put it. Like the professional manager, the civil servant pursues his career within an occupational milieu that restricts his vision and duties to the practical tasks in hand: which is in itself a demand for the acceptance of existing social forms. 'Power is to be found more in uneventful routine than in conscious and active exercise of will' (Westergaard and Resler 1975:144).

Politics and Consensus

The missing theory of elites is closely connected with another major lacuna in end-of-ideologism, namely, how dominant-class interests can be reconciled with the democratic political order which could in principle threaten them. The answer, Lipset argues, is that legitimacy is the foundation of democratic states, expressed as consensus among the citizens on overarching (or 'underlying') values (Lipset 1963:83). Empirically, this claim is quickly disposed of. Ample survey research in American society during the 1950s – which is where end-of-ideologism blossomed – demonstrated quite high levels of political distrust among respondents. For example, in 1958 one quarter felt that 'quite a few' politicians were crooks (Hamilton and Wright 1975:29). At the very best, the pattern of responses could only be interpreted as indicating widespread apathy and incomprehension among the public concerning political processes. 'What we have here, then,' Hamilton and Wright (1975:31) point out, 'is not theorising in the *absence* of fact, but theorising in wholesale *disregard* of facts which were both relevant and readily available.'

Allowing that a large measure of passive acquiescence is a reasonable description of popular faith in democracy, there is a more important theoretical objection to this consensual model. Given the highly unequal distribution of the resources needed to mobilise public opinion, it must be acknowledged that such agreement on values as does exist is unlikely to be 'a kind of independent convergence in the moral outlook of different classes' (Parkin 1972:81). It is an expression of ideological control, of processes of legitimation which encourage people, in however ambivalent and incomplete a fashion, to accept capitalism as a way of life. (On this, see especially Miliband 1969:chs. 7 & 8.) It is not possible here to develop this line of argument, but the usual disclaimer needs to be made. That is, what is at stake in this debate is not primarily the capacity of elites to carry out the systematic indoctrination of the disprivileged. It is that powerful institutionalised pressures enshrine the values of elite groups, with the effect of crowding out 'unofficial', radical versions of social reality. In the mass media, for example, the relationship between ownership and editorial policy may go some way, in some instances, towards explaining lack of sympathy with organised labour. But equally efficacious in the long run are the anonymous pressures of advertisers, and far more discreet. And what is not said is in the end just as important as what is. The schools, to take another example, are not places necessarily where civic obedience is consciously inculcated by representatives of the dominant classes. And yet they are likely to be extremely influential in bringing about the covert socialisation of working-class children for lowly occupational status. Certainly, Mann points out (1970:436-7), the curriculum-content offers little in the way of points of reference for the understanding of society as it appears in working-class experience. Under such conditions, the development of political radicalism must be regarded as extremely questionable. The point is not that organised opposition has *no* effect, but that to question the basic principles of the existing order is liable to appear as either utopian or downright subversive. The ideological forces contributing to stability and continuity do not have to be constantly mobilised over specific issues, or at each election time, as is the case with oppositional parties. They are built into the routine, day-to-day functioning of capitalist societies.

Working-class values, Parkin therefore argues (1972:81 ff.), can only be understood in relation to a *dominant* meaning-system. This moral framework for the interpretation of inequalities, if wholly articulated and endorsed, leads logically either to the conceptualisation of the social order in hierarchical, status terms; or to a belief in the virtues of competitive individualism. Since the specific values derived from this framework are so ubiquitous and insidiously diffused, it could be expected that elements of it shape the outlook of the working class as a whole. Nonetheless, the ideological hegemony of dominant values is qualified only, for since they

> 'are the moral representation of the interests and opportunities of more privileged groups, their "appropriateness" as far as the less privileged are concerned is problematic.

> The tendency among the underprivileged is not to reject these values, and thus to create an entirely different normative system, but to negotiate or modify them in the light of their own existential conditions' (Parkin 1972: 92).

In this sense then the working-class meaning is typically a *subordinate* one. Unlike the third, *radical* meaning-system, it has no fixed points of reference which could bring it direct ideological confrontation with the publicly approved images of society by which the working class is beset. It is a form of what Lenin called 'trade-union consciousness', which cannot be usefully thought of in terms of a single level of meaning. In abstract evaluational contexts, pollsters and sociologists tend to tap essentially 'second-hand' opinions handed down by the dominant classes. In concrete situations involving *action* the subordinate meaning-system provides the frame of reference. It supports the idea of collective class action, but entertains doubts about the legitimacy even of this when pushed beyond the limits of what is 'reasonable' in the opinion of a faceless but omnipresent 'public'. And as Michael Frayn has neatly remarked public opinion on this question seems quite clear. It 'unquestioningly concedes the right of men in a free society to withdraw their labour. It just draws the line at strikes'. (See his humorous but extremely incisive piece in Blackburn and Cockburn eds., 1967.)

The postulation of a subordinate working-class meaning-system has a very great heuristic value, and fits within the logic of a 'ruling class', or 'power elite', model of capitalist societies. It moves the argument about working-class values away from the quite spurious 'conflict versus consensus' controversy in the analysis of class, where in fact it should never have been allowed to drift in the first place. As Parkin explicitly acknowledges, the idea of a subordinate meaning-system derives from Marx's contention that ruling-class power always takes on a normative as well as a factual aspect: this is what class domination means. More specifically, the notion provides a means of expressing in analytical form Weber's scepticism about the probability that market conflicts will take on a politicised stamp of the kind entailed by the Marxian definition of class consciousness. Nevertheless, working-class subordination can be broken, and the conditions under which this might occur are the subject of the final chapter. There is, however, a logically prior theme to be taken up. However problematical the radicalisation of the working class, that of the middle classes is still more so. The stability of democratic politics has been to a large extent underwritten by the emergence of certain occupational strata on which conservative and liberal parties have been able to rely for support. In more general terms, the acceptance of dominant definitions of social reality has found relatively few barriers among these groups, and the reasons for this have an obvious general relevance to the explanation of cleavage and conflict in contemporary western states.

4 Working-class and middle-class worlds

Sociologists conventionally — because it is an operationally useful thing to do — draw a line within the propertyless stratum, distinguishing as 'middle class' a hotch-potch of occupational groups which in many ways have very little in common with one another. Although a social class in terms of Weber's definition, the middle classes are best understood as comprising a residual category. They do not, as a matter of definition, have the collective control of decision-making available to elite groups. However, it is often helpful to refer to an 'upper-middle' class, since they provide the principal recruitment strata for elite groups (Giddens 1974:15). On the other hand, the middle classes do not on balance share the social and political attitudes of the working class either. Despite the changes wrought by political and technological innovations in the twentieth century, it still makes sense, Goldthorpe and Lockwood argue (1963:147), to see the two classes as characterised by significantly different normative perspectives (see over).

These perspectives are subject to all the usual qualifications attached to ideal-typical constructions. They represent a point of departure for analysis, not the orderly and coherent outlook of the average members of a class.

'Working class' and 'manual workers' are interchangeable expressions, but no simple definition of either is possible in

	Working class perspective	*Middle class perspective*
General beliefs	The social order is divided into 'us' and 'them': those who do not have authority and those who do. The division between 'us' and 'them' is virtually fixed, at least from the point of view of one man's life chances. What happens to you depends a lot on luck; otherwise you have to learn to put up with things.	The social order is a hierarchy of differentially rewarded positions: a ladder containing many rungs. It is possible for individuals to move from one level of the hierarchy to another. Those who have ability and initiative can overcome obstacles and create their own opportunities. Where a man ends up depends on what he makes of himself.
General values	'We' ought to stick together and get what we can as a group. You may as well enjoy yourself while you can instead of trying to make yourself 'a cut above the rest'.	Every man ought to make the most of his own capabilities and be responsible for his own welfare. You cannot expect to get anywhere in the world if you squander your time and money. 'Getting on' means making sacrifices.
Attitudes on more specific issues	(on the best job for a son) 'A trade in his hands'. 'A good steady job'. (towards people needing social assistance) 'They have been unlucky'. 'They never had a chance'. 'It could happen to any of us'. (on Trade unions) 'Trade Unions are the only means workers have of protecting themselves and of improving their standard of living'.	'As good a start as you can give him'. 'A job that leads somewhere'. 'Many of them had the same opportunities as others who have managed well enough'. 'They are a burden on those who are trying to help themselves'. 'Trade Unions have too much power in the country'. 'The Unions put the interests of a section before the interests of the nation as a whole'.

terms of occupational groupings. The middle and working classes are differentiated by quite complex criteria, but the term 'manual' derives from the fact that this class of employees is directly engaged in the physical creation and delivery of goods and services. A consequence of this fact is that manual workers stand in a very direct relationship to the market for labour. Whenever an unseen and anonymous public cuts down its consumption of jam, or stops buying new cars, their market chances come under threat in a manner not typical of most middle-class employment. There are two related features of the class situation of workers worth mentioning here: they do not possess skills for which a lengthy education and/or occupational training are required, and they are not an integral part of the authority hierarchy of the work organisation which employs them. The working class is made up of operatives, as opposed to administrators and decision-makers. However, this is all that can be usefully said in a general way about the differences between the two classes. The object of this chapter is to make these very compressed remarks clearer.

Marx noted the growth of the 'new' (i.e., non-propertied) middle class without trying to make a distinct place for it in his theory of class conflict. There cannot be a middle class in the revolutionary transformation of capitalist society, and Marx has little to say about why an important line of cleavage should make its appearance within the propertyless stratum. Weber's more extended definition of class helps in this context, and Lockwood has used it to help explain why clerical employees in Britain have always been socially and politically isolated from the working class. Clerks are a critical occupational group, since clerks are apparently close to manual workers in terms of their class attributes, and what can be shown about them applies *a fortiori* to the more privileged non-manual occupations. Historically, the gulf between manual and even the most modest white-collar employment has been one of the most striking features of the class order in British society. The divide is far from bridged nowadays, even though there has been a proliferation of clerical posts employing people with relatively low earnings, and with humble scholastic and vocational qualifications. What particularly attracted Lockwood's interest was the assertion sometimes made by marxists that the clerks were a classical illustration of the concept of 'false consciousness', a phrase coined by Engels in another context. That is, the clerks' espousal of middle-class values was held to be contrary to their 'real' interests against private property.

The fact is, Lockwood demonstrates, that the class position of the clerk is not the same as that of manual workers. He makes a now widely-used distinction between 'market' and 'work' situation, though both are subsumed under the heading of 'class'. The market situation does not mean *income* solely, and especially not the contents of a weekly pay packet. In terms of security of income, freedom from the threat of unemployment, opportunities for promotion to more lucrative positions, and special sickness and pension benefits, clerical work has great advantages over manual labour. A particularly striking example concerns the estimation of real incomes. Lockwood passes relatively lightly over this for lack of empirical evidence, but obviously we should take this form of income (*hidden* income because it never appears in the tax returns) very seriously indeed, as the following table indicates. Referred to often simply as 'perks', or 'fringe benefits', these terms are somewhat lighthearted in view of their impact on the real-life market situation of the recipients. It is true that clerical people share in only a fairly minor way in these perks, but this, combined with the other elements in their relationship to the structure of rewards marks them off definitively from manual workers.

Table 4.1 Fringe benefits as a percentage of non-manual salaries (England, 1966)

£1,000 per year	11%
£1,600 per year	15%
£3,500 per year	19%
£4,200 per year	21%
£7,000 plus per year	31%

Source: Martin & Crouch, 1971:252. (Original source: *The Economist*, 27/8/1966)

No less important in the formation of contrasting class attitudes is the day-to-day experience of the workplace — the work situation, which Lockwood defines as the 'the set of social relationships in which the individual is involved at work by virtue of his position in the division of labour'. Here he is harking back to Marx, who stressed much more firmly than Weber the unifying influence of the factory system on the working class.

'The establishment of machine production in factories and the rationalisation of organisation which this entailed created a working environment which was highly conducive to the emergence of class-conscious action. Productive

> relationships in the factory separated management from the worker as they simultaneously united workers with one another in cohesive groups. Physical separation and concentration were reinforced socially by the impersonal discipline and standardised relationships of the factory bureaucracy; and these were further generalised through the operation of the labour market. In this way the factory became, in Michels' phrase, a model school of working-class solidarity' (Lockwood, 1958:71).

Historically, the clerical worker has experienced nothing like this degree of regimentation. The social relationships of the modern office have remained relatively personalised. Lateness, a day or two off sick, or a visit to the dentist during working hours, are all likely to be more sympathetically regarded than in the case of manual workers. Moreover, the office setting provides the contact with status superiors which reinforces the clerk's sense of distance from manual workers, symbolised by separate entrances and timekeeping methods for 'staff' and 'works' personnel, segregated canteen and toilet facilities, and suchlike; even the possibilities of contact between routine non-manual and manual personnel are reduced to a minimum by the physical distance normally found between the production plants and the administrative building. Most important of all, direct exchanges between clerks and workers are likely to involve the formers as a representative of managerial authority, which could hardly be the basis for a solidary social grouping across the manual/non-manual line. And of course the majority of clerks are employed in organisations where there are no manual workers anyway.

Unquestionably, clerical work does not have the advantages it once held in the eyes of ambitious working-class parents. In the nineteenth century the market value of the clerk's services was assured by his command of the scarce skill of literacy. By the same token, clerking work attracted a socially superior type, the sons of well-to-do or even bourgeois families who came to learn the business. In the mid-twentieth century, blackcoated employees had to face up to the unpalatable fact that mass education had stripped them of their prime bargaining asset. They had become the common labourers of the middle class, ranking only above unskilled manual workers in terms of occupational training received. As the market advantages of the group declined, so did its social prestige, a process hastened by the infiltration of manual workers' children and of women, who by 1951 made up three out of every five clerks. Changes in the work situation accompanied this decline. These changes were uniformly in the direction of bureaucratisation, which in turn reacted upon chances of occupational mobility. The sub-division and multiplication of administrative tasks has extended the ratio of ancillary to managerial personnel, so limiting the possibility of promotion. In some cases, it has also robbed non-manual employment of many intrinsic rewards — autonomy, variegated problems, and the sense of being an integral part of the social system of the office and of an authority hierarchy. To a much greater extent than was once the case, the shop-floor organisation of the factory finds its clerical analogue in serried rows of machine operators performing routine functions.

Table 4.2 Pension provision for employees, British manufacturing Industry, 1968

	(1) Operatives	(2) Admin. tech., clerical staff	(2) as percent of (1)
Percent of employees covered	37%	56%	151
Average expenditure per employee:			
Overall (incl. those not covered)	£14·4	£79·1	549
For those covered, only	£43·6	£141·3	324

Source: Westergaard and Resler 1975:90

These developments have resulted in a partial abandonment of the clerk's 'traditional' reluctance to unionise. In general,

Lockwood suggests (1958:142), bureaucratisation has been to the blackcoated workforce what factory organisation and the labour market have been to the manual worker – a source of solidarity. It is important not to overstate this growth in clerical class consciousness. At the time of the study, only about a quarter of all clerks were in unions, and in the intervening period this proportion has not changed much. Nonetheless, to the extent that a clear division exists between 'managerial' and 'clerical' grades by reason of the organisation of work and blocked mobility, then unionism is a likely outcome. The latter factor, especially, seems to be a crucial one. Sykes (1965) discovered that of 96 clerks he interviewed in a Scottish steel firm 92 were opposed to the idea of unions for themselves, though not for manual workers. As one clerk put it succinctly, they could expect to gain more for themselves through individual than through collective action. During the course of the study, however, management introduced a trainee scheme for higher posts of the sort common in large-scale enterprises. As a result, all the clerks joined a union. Wherever formal educational qualifications, rather than on-the-job training, become the criteria for promotion the traditional loyalty of the clerk to the firm comes under strain. Such loyalty depends on a paternalistic relationship between employee and employer, and not surprisingly it is in the vast government bureaucracies that clerical unionisation has made the greatest strides. About 70 percent of their employees are union members. In the distributive trades, where small firms and administrative particularism prevail, only 13 percent are unionised (Raynor 1969:56, table 15). In some ways, then, the process of bureaucratisation has affected the class situation of the clerk in a fashion analogous to that which overtook the manual workforce much earlier in the history of capitalism.

Nonetheless, it would appear that the 'proletarianisation' of the routine white-collar employee has distinct structural limits. Despite all the changes which have taken place, he remains part of the authority hierarchy and continues to share considerable advantages because of that fact. It has to be remembered, first of all, that only *some* manual work offers parity of income, and when hidden income is also taken into account, the clerk has clear advantages. Moreover, administrative employees enjoy annual increments and periodic rises which, like those of their superiors, depend on the income of the work organisation as a whole. This highlights the fact that the *principles* of income formation are discontinuous between manual and non-manual occupations generally. Such narrowing of differentials as has occurred can be traced chiefly to the expansion in capitalist economies, which has raised manual incomes through greater productivity. This isolation from the pressures of the labour market is even more obvious in the case of that high proportion of clerical people located in work organisations such as banks and government agencies, which are not directly dependent on the market, but it applies in the productive sector too. This fundamental difference in class situation becomes most obvious during times of slump. In the United States during the thirties the decline in salaries was very much less than that in wages, and the incidence of unemployment among the middle class in 1930 was 4 percent, as against 10-13 percent among manual workers (Mills 1956:280-1). Even productive enterprises shed administrative labour much less readily than their manual workers, whose level of pay and security of employment alike are tied closely to physical output.

Furthermore, it would be unwise to conclude that trends in career mobility are universally working to the disadvantage of the routine non-manual stratum. The evidence on this is somewhat contradictory, itself a fact of some importance. Of lower white-collar employees in one study 86 percent stated that a person of ability could hope to reach middle management, and a quarter of them thought that progress even beyond this point was possible (Goldthorpe *et al.* 1969:76). Indeed, common sense suggests that the increasing complexity and differentiation characteristic of administrative bureaucracies may actually create new, albeit limited, career paths. Within the accounts, sales or personnel departments, for example, quite intricate sub-hierarchies may form. Nor is movement between them necessarily precluded, since beyond a certain point the division of labour impairs efficiency in decision-making. A similar observation has been made in a study of the effects of mechanisation on office work, to the effect that,

> 'what these machines really replaced was a great deal of laborious manual effort in checking data and routine arithmetical calculations...some understanding of the business continued to be the desirable qualification of the clerical worker, whether his work was done by manual or mechanical means' (quoted by Giddens 1973:194).

There does seem, in fact, to be a point beyond which the rationalisation of administration cannot go without becoming self-defeating. Even a copy-typist or a stenographer exercises symbolic skills of an order not required for manual work, and the value of those skills is greatly enhanced by some understanding of the overall functioning of the office. Certainly, there is a white-collar 'proletariat' (largely recruited from women nowadays), and formal education is increasingly necessary for the highest posts in large organisations. But the extent of this change needs to be kept firmly in proportion. There is no reason to believe that *long-range* career mobility has ever been a major feature of routine non-manual employment, and it continues to provide a level of security, rewards, and modest advancement which is not typical of the mass of working-class occupations. The fact, Lockwood concludes, that the clerk has become more marginal to the middle class, that to some extent the mid-twentieth century saw for the first time the articulation of clerical class-consciousness, is not to say that he is of the working class. This is particularly evident in the character of blackcoated unionism, which has taken manual unions as a model of organisation, but still operates in a distinctive style in its dealings with employers. For instance, clerks have been by no means averse to affiliation with the T.U.C. However, this cooperation with labour has been notably greater on the instrumental rather than on the overtly ideological plane, the question of direct support for the Labour Party (for example) being a highly contentious issue. This middle-of-the road unionism accurately reflects the conflicting pressures within the class situation of clerical labour. Clerks are themselves increasingly drawn from working-class backgrounds, and organise collectively to bargain with their employers. On the other hand, their market interests do not predispose them to radical hostility to the principles of reward allocation, but to fight for a more favourable share within the existing rules. Collectivism, moreover, can be easily undermined by the possibility and hope of individual mobility. Their situation, therefore, cannot be understood in terms of a simple dichotomy.

This last observation draws attention to the difficulty of speaking of *the* middle class, except in the context of comparisons with the working class. The non-manual stratum is differentiated to an extent not really matched by the ranks of manual labour. Incomes will serve as an illustration. In the United States, manual workers cluster tightly between the fifth and eighth income-tenths, while white-collar occupations straddle the entire span between the first and sixth income-tenths (Kolko 1962:85), and even this probably underestimates the range. In terms of work situation, too, the range is enormous, from the girl in the typing pool to the diversity and autonomy of private legal practice. There are many gradations of the 'middle-class perspective', therefore, and for that reason it is perhaps better to speak in terms of a plurality of groups, the middle classes. What they do have in common, however, is their attachment to a meritocratic social philosophy, a belief in personal qualities, individual effort and learning as the key to occupational success, and in 'achievement' as the basis of social-honour ascription. In the most general terms, it could be said that the differences within the middle class as a whole are rooted in the fact that for the lower-middle classes the proof of the pudding still lies in the future. It is for this reason that they tend to out-Herod Herod, to be more concerned (sometimes) with 'respectability', to harrass their children more about their progress at school, and very often to make striking sacrifices to put their offspring through extended education. Their concern for these values really cannot (as Lockwood stresses) be *explained* in terms of 'snobbishness', even though that may be present in their attitudes. The distinctive 'traditional' reluctance of the clerk to unionise

> 'cannot be dismissed by a facile reference to the snobbishness of the clerk. His status situation is only one aspect of his total class situation, and on the whole it has been of secondary importance in his class outlook and collective action, reinforcing rather than undermining the experiences which have their origins in his economic position and working contacts' (Lockwood 1958:198).

The lower-middle-class person frequently and perhaps increasingly finds himself in a socially marginal position. He can go 'down' or 'up', and there are compelling psychological and practical reasons why he should not wish the first alternative, despite all the changes in routine non-manual occupations. Collective action, however, implies that individual solutions to the class predicament are useless, and seen to be so. This is by no means universally the case. Furthermore, by reason of his work situation, the routine non-manual employee is not exposed daily to norms and practices which denigrate the value of self-help and individualism. A particular occupational location does not automatically confer middle-class values — the personal conflicts of loyalty frequently experienced by the upwardly mobile illustrate this fact. However, non-manual employment does at least normally ensure the absence of the collective resistance to middle-class values so often found among working-class groups. For instance, Sykes (1965:308) found that among the manual workers in his sample promotion to the rank of foreman was regarded as a form of class treachery. The whole legitimating ideology of the office-worker, on the contrary, rests on the premise that routine non-manual employees are the competent, reliable and indispensable aids of the administrative hierarchy; and that therefore they are entitled, as well as able, to take on more responsible functions within the organisation. One could say that to be middle class is to internalise the dominant meaning-system of capitalist society, with its strong emphasis on the virtues of competitive individualism.

Another way of expressing the contrast between working-

and middle-class employment is to say that the manual worker sells his labour by the week, whereas even the petty bureaucrat trades in his services for a lifetime (Rex 1961:140). It is the difference between a 'job' and a 'career'. The logic of a 'career', especially if the idea is extended beyond the lifetime of a single individual, underlies the middle-class success in the planning and preparation necessary to achieve the long-term goal of occupational success. Not only does the orderliness and stability of a career provide a secure material background, but it provides the middle-class parent with first-hand knowledge of the social milieu in which formal education, deftness in interpersonal relations, and self-confidence are at a premium. These values are readily passed on during the early socialisation of children, often in a quite unconscious way. Kohn (1969:190) has pointed out that autonomy, complexity of task, and the degree to which task-performance permits a number of solutions, all of which are aspects of the work situation, are associated with attitudes of self-reliance and self-direction. As he observed in an earlier paper (Kohn 1963), the connection made between class-based differences in child rearing practices, parental education and divergent values, is probably an indirect and contingent one. Whether they take Dr. Spock or their own grandmothers as the guide to *method*, the *values* are implicit in middle-class culture. The very idea that a child can be 'developed' in a purposeful way to secure its own future is quintessentially a middle-class one.

Once again, the routine white-collar stratum is differentiated from both manual workers and the established middle classes with respect to the cluster of values which prescribe and ensure occupational advancement. In their aspirations for their children and in their faith that these aspirations will be fulfilled they are quite distinct from the working class and higher non-manual groups, but on the whole lean decisively towards the latter. Martin (1954:171-2) found that 64.2 percent of clerical parents felt strongly about their children going to grammar school, as against 58.5 percent and 47.0 percent of skilled and unskilled workers. 80 percent of the 'professional' category felt this way. However,

49.4 percent of the professionals and a quarter of the clerks stated that they would send the child elsewhere, while only a handful of the workers took this very decisive attitude. Perhaps the most convincing demonstration of 'middle-classness' however, was in the pattern of responses given by those parents who, having expressed a preference for grammar school, were asked about their preferences for post-secondary education. 58.8 percent of the clerical group chose university or professional training, substantially more than the professionals, 44.8 percent. Only 23 percent of skilled workers chose this option, and 14.2 percent of unskilled parents. The gap between ambition and performance would no doubt be considerable, but the mere fact that the clerical parents took such a strong line over their children's future is instructive. Some degree of ideological overkill is perhaps inevitable to ensure that a somewhat uncertain outcome is not rendered more so by an initial failure of commitment to the goal.

Soundings among the 'solid' middle classes — professionals and business people — suggest that they see the working class in no very favourable light (Deverson and Lindsay 1975:ch.9). This is an important area of class studies which has been very much neglected. Such people may well exercise a critical influence on class attitudes, since it is through them that role stereotypes and social imagery are mediated. To the working class, such people are remote both socially and at the workplace, contacts being limited essentially to official encounters. To the lower-middle class and the socially mobile, however, their values and attitudes are of immediate significance, both from the point of view of day-to-day interaction and career prospects. Work in the world of the middle classes is virtually never a relationship between the individual and an object or a task, such as making ballbearings or delivering letters. It involves cooperation with, and acceptance by, colleagues and bosses. Much of the function of socialisation is performed by the educational system, but the principle remains good that movement from a working-class to a middle-class environment involves a considerable normative shift. Deverson and Lindsay found that a few, notably those who have links with the working class, can put their own situation in perspective and sympathise with the relative deprivation of manual employment. For most, the worker-with-car seems to sum up their conception of the class order. The working class tends to be pigeon-holed as less hard-working and less able than the middle class. Some think workers earn more than their due, and that the rich who 'give jobs to the poor' (as one respondent expressed it) are under-valued by a misplaced egalitarian ethos, and persecuted by unjust redistributive measures. Many resent the slight sense of unease with which they enjoy their good fortune. One woman with two daughters at an exclusive private school insisted,

> 'If we're prepared to pay for the school fees, well, that's our business really. I don't go round telling my daily that I'm paying rates to put her children through school' (Deverson and Lindsay 1975:195).

Even through the more guarded judgments there runs a strong sense of status differentiation, to the effect that the social classes do not easily mix and cannot be expected to. Although overt hostility to the working class is not always in evidence, there is a strong sense of social distance detectable in these responses, combined with a considerable belief in the essential rightfulness of their own favoured position in the scheme of things. These particular middle-class people were strikingly ignorant of the scope of inequality, and definitely nourished strong delusions about the extent of working-class affluence. They objected to state interference in social life, and were convinced that taxes were never used to help them. Above all, their attitudes were predicated on the (usually unspoken) assumption that the social order is a field of limitless opportunity for the individual of talent and will. It rarely occurred to anyone to draw the inescapable conclusion, that a competitive world necessarily throws up more losers than winners. Just how typical these rather militant opinions are of the middle class as a whole are is difficult to say in the absence of systematic research. At any rate, they throw into relief certain features commonly met with in the middle-class outlook, such as hostility to the allegedly overweening power of trade unions and to what they see as retrograde developments in the extension of the welfare state. Probably a quite active resentment lies close to the surface, since the middle classes never lack political spokesmen to draw invidious comparisons with working-class affluence.

Middle-class Radicals

Nevertheless, members of the middle classes also provide much of the leadership and ideology of social-democratic parties. They contribute the lion's share of support for reformist pressure groups (such as consumer associations), and for 'third' parties, such as the Liberals in Britain and the Values party in New Zealand. Some of these activities are obviously compatible with conservatism in both the political and ideological sense, but equally some are not. While not usually left-wing in the conventional meaning of the phrase, these middle-class groups quite often introduce new themes and issues into political life, in such a way as to challenge vested interests and stir up social passions.

Parkin's (1968) study of the Campaign for Nuclear Disarmament, which galvanised British political life around 1960, deals with one such movement. C.N.D. harboured communists and anarchists, churchmen and ideologically unattached intellectuals, and the sole unifying aim of this improbable coalition was to force a government commitment to the unilateral renunciation of nuclear weapons. However, its followers did also have one common social characteristic, that they were recruited chiefly from the educated, professional middle classes. Pursuing an argument developed by Parsons (1952,1968), Parkin therefore considered the possibility that the institutionalised values associated respectively with 'business' and 'professional' roles might predispose the latter group more to the kind of moral stance which C.N.D. involvement symbolised for many of its adherents. In that case, one might have to start thinking in terms of a line of vertical differentiation within the established middle classes. But, at least in the case of this particular form of middle-class dissent, the dichotomy is too crude to be useful.

It was true the C.N.D-ers were concentrated in 'nonbusiness' occupations, for reasons which seem fairly straightforward. A career in industry and commerce entails a continuous process of socialisation and selection common to all bureaucratic organisations in its essential features. The profit-making institutions of corporate capitalism, especially, embody the conservative values of their dominant interests. Demonstrated competence in the job is no doubt an important criterion of advancement, but so is the ability to make one's face fit, and to be not simply able but eager in the performance of duties. As Whyte's label has it, the ambitious executive must become an organisation man, and the Pahls (1971:184), among others, have documented the willy-nilly inclusion of managerial couples in social circles of work acquaintances, sometimes resulting in fairly severe strains on them. Refusal to enter the circle, or unease in it, are just the signs which this mechanism is intended to detect — it is a classic instance of status-group formation. The consistent obtrusion of 'deviant' opinions, let alone actually marching on an American base in very dubious company, would in all likelihood entail a high cost in career terms. Of course, there will always be individual exceptions — C.N.D. did include the odd company director. On the whole, though, the world of business attracts and keeps 'realists' who find overt dissent uncomfortable, even where this is not linked with a left-wing political programme.

The 'professionals', however, do not constitute a satisfactory contrasting category.

> 'It is not sufficient to claim merely that middle-class radicals will be found in the professions as a sanctuary shielding them from direct involvement in capitalism (narrowly defined) since professional workers are increasingly found in the employment of private industry. Instead, it must be further predicted that radicals will seek to offer their professional services to organisations and institutions of a non-commercial, non-profit-making type, and will avoid employment in settings where professional values are threatened by the business ethics of capitalism'.

Thus, the clustering of middle-class radicals in certain

occupations is best explained as

> 'the result of occupational self-selection on the part of radicals, stemming from their desire to avoid direct employment in capitalist economic institutions' (Parkin 1968:188-9).

This puts a quite different complexion on the argument. The crucial fact about these dissenters is not their 'professional' status as such, but their common wish to find a working environment in which they will not be subjected to the pressures of values greatly at odds with their own. Their broadly similar occupational status could be seen as much an effect as a cause of a personal commitment to social reform, which activism in C.N.D. expressed.

Table 4.3 The middle classes in the United States, 1870-1940

	1870	1940
Old middle class	*85%*	*44%*
Farmers	62	23
Businessmen	21	19
Free professionals	2	2
% of labour force	*33*	*20*
New middle class	*15%*	*56%*
Managers	2	6
Salaried professionals	4	14
Salespeople	7	14
Office workers	2	22
% of labour force	*6*	*25*

Source: Mills 1951:63,65

The trend has been overwhelmingly towards the *salaried* employment of professionally qualified people, something which in itself ought to caution us against attaching overmuch significance to the label. In any case, professional autonomy, based on a fee rather than salaried employment, does not automatically create the basis for divergent values within the middle class. Law and accountancy illustrate the point. One can acknowledge the part played by lawyers in maintaining civil and political liberties without losing sight of the fact that the law serves the classes in very different ways. Most legal work, and especially its most lucrative part, lies in the field of property-related adjudication — this is true even of the solicitor, the general practitioner. Lawyers are a key link in the relationship between corporate capitalism and the state, and the dominant entrepreneurial ethos of the profession reflects this simple fact. This is even more apt a characterisation of accountancy, which was in a straightforward sense the creation of capitalist enterprise. Both the content of accountancy practice, and the circumstances in which the accountant's skills are bought and sold, bind him firmly to the values of the business community. This sort of reasoning underlies Parkin's distinction between 'business' and 'welfare and creative professions'. Under the latter heading he included (1968:180) 'social work, medical services, teaching, the church, journalism, art, architecture, scientific research and so on'. Again, the argument is not that these occupations typically produce radicals. Of the solid middle classes in Britain 85 percent vote Conservative (Blondel 1967:57), and even the 10 percent who vote Labour could hardly be categorised as radical for that reason. The point is simply that this constellation of professions appears especially congenial to certain personalities.

Just what combination of influences produce the middle-class radical is very difficult to say. The educated middle classes themselves have always stressed the liberating effect of disinterested knowledge on the individual — J.S. Mill was perhaps the greatest liberal exponent of this point of view. It is found again in sociological dress in Mannheim's 'socially unattached intelligentsia', a group in which 'a common educational heritage progressively tends to suppress differences of birth, status, profession, and wealth, and to unite the individual educated person on the basis of the education they have received' (Mannheim 1960:138). 'Education', however, suffers from the same sort of vagueness as 'professionalism'. Certain *specific* educational experiences would seem to be associated with middle-class dissent, namely university training in the humanities and social sciences. These subjects provide a more systematic and critical view of society than is true of, say, engineering and medicine. In contrast to secondary education, Parkin suggests (1968: 171-2), the conflicts of values and opinions found in the university setting can for some students amount to a re-socialising experience. Selective schools — from which the young C.N.D. supporters mostly came — propagate a much more narrowly middle-class social frame of reference, which is likely to come under fire during the student years. Of course, all shades of received opinion may be shaken by extended education, but the shift in the student body is likely to be in a libertarian and politically leftward direction as they approach graduation. In the C.N.D. sample, the bias according to academic specialisms was extremely heavy: 70 percent of those in higher education were studying arts and social sciences, 17 percent pure and applied science. This ratio is not particularly surprising in view of the findings of other studies of student attitudes, and has obvious implications for the occupational destinations of C.N.D. youth. Simple deductions from these shared educational histories, however, would be out of place. Although the university, for many, is a radicalising milieu, the same marked predilection for 'ideological' subjects of study was found among those who had not yet entered higher education, pointing once more to a complementary process of self-selection. There is more than a hint that the propensity to political activism is inherited from parents to some extent, but this merely pushes the problem back one generation. The question 'what makes a middle-class radical?' stirs up very difficult issues concerning the interaction of personality and social structure which cannot be pursued here.

From a theoretical standpoint, a feature of Parkin's study is its function in drawing attention to the limitations on generalisation about the link between class position and meaning-system. This form of middle-class protest cannot possibly be understood in terms of class interests resting on material and social deprivation. On the contrary, it arose from an unusually *strong* moral commitment to the liberal and humanitarian values of capitalist society. Consequently, C.N.D-ers on the whole were distinctly cool towards institutionalised politics — including the Labour party — and the inevitable compromises demanded by the structure of power. For this reason alone, certain reservations have to be entertained about assimilating one form of middle-class 'deviance' to another without a suitably rigorous investigation of both. Nevertheless, it is suggestive to find a somewhat similar skewing in the occupational status of the parliamentary wings of the two major parties:

> 'The Labour middle class is mainly composed of three groups, the teachers, the journalists, and the lawyers; other middle-class occupations are represented only by a few members each. The Conservative parliamentary party, on the other hand, has scarcely any teachers. Farmers and regular soldiers are more numerous than journalists and publicists. Lawyers and businessmen are more numerous than any two of these groups together. In the Labour party, the middle class is primarily a middle class of intellectuals or, at any rate, a middle class which can be distinguished from the manual working class and the white-collar workers because it discusses ideas, not because it makes money. In the Conservative party, the intellectual middle class exists, but it is in a small minority' (Blondel 1967:140).

The contrast is most striking with respect to business connections. In the parliaments he studied Blondel found that a third of Conservative M.P.s started in business, while 60 percent eventually had business connections irrespective of their initial occupation. Only 10 percent of the Labour party were involved with business.

Observe that the most useful line of cleavage within the established middle classes is still a *horizontal* one. The law is commonly regarded as the epitome of a 'profession', but sociologically the term is hopelessly ambiguous, since it is applied to a range of occupations which have absolutely nothing in common. This point is made forcibly by Johnson

(1972:45-7), who suggests that 'professionalism' can best be conceptualised as a peculiar form of occupational control. The content of the job, or its practitioners' ideology, are not the issue. What is relevant is that some occupational groups manage to effect corporate, legal closure of opportunities, so determining who shall practise what. Esoteric knowledge plays an important part in such closure, forming both a justification and a basis for autonomy in recruitment and training. Unquestionably, however, the emphasis of 'professional' ideologies on long training and technical expertise serves to create manpower scarcity and economic monopolies, however much they may be argued to be essential to good practice. For example, house conveyancing and divorces involve complicated procedures and documentation which cause people often to leave the business to lawyers even where it is not obligatory to do so. But this is not to say that the procedures could not be made simpler. The ability of the occupation to conserve its autonomy under conditions of change in the content of practice, or in the face of pressure from organised groups of clients, depends essentially on its relationship to the power structure.

Doctors in America have been extremely successful in this respect. Despite the immense expansion in medical needs caused by two world wars and social progress generally, Mills points out (1956:119), there was in 1940 one licensed physician to every 750 people in the United States, where in 1900 the ratio was 1:578. During those years the general practitioner has largely handed over responsibility for serious cases to the hospitals, where once he was diagnostician, nurse and comforter all rolled into one. Yet he has preserved a central and lucrative role as gatekeeper in the system of health care, although the scientific division of labour has created a hierarchy within the profession, controlled by specialists through their privileged access to hospital facilities. Entrepreneurship has found a new home in the hospital bureaucracy. The 'sick market' is managed by informal cliques, and with it the career chances of new entrants to the physicians' ranks (Mills 1956:117). In Britain, the development of the health services has followed a somewhat different path, largely owing to state intervention. The compromise between government and the profession there had the effect of institutionally defining the hospital as an extension of general practice, with correspondingly less encroachment on the rewards and authority of that branch of the occupation. There are, however, tensions endemic in this situation, as the militancy of junior hospital doctors is making increasingly clear. In both countries, the lack of growth in the profession has only been possible because of physician control over the specialised skills wielded by nurses, radiographers, dietiticians and so on, which in turn severely limits the possibility of the professionalisation of those occupations, in Johnson's sense of the word.

In fact, the occupations which first spring to mind when the word 'profession' is mentioned are the most entrepreneurially organised and controlled, which is unlikely to align them with the social and political values of the left. The personal altruism of the individual practitioner is not an issue in this case. The question is to whom the services of the professional are available and under what conditions. Both medicine and law have been notable for their resistance to state intervention in the allocation of services, and the 'family business' aspect of their internal organisation is strong. Children following their fathers' occupation is a very marked feature of the 'higher professions' (cf. Kelsall 1954). Not surprisingly, the greater the degree of occupational closure, the heavier the class bias in recruitment, law being in this respect even more exclusive than the bureaucracies of the state and economy. Where the state steps in to provide a service for a mass public, a different ethos and organisation is created. Teaching is the outstanding example here. Because they form a huge occupational group, and because the state pays their salaries, the teacher are 'the economic proletarians of the professions' (Mills 1956:129). In turn, teaching has everywhere been a traditional avenue of social ascent for working-class children. The bureaucratic organisation of the educational services and poor opportunities for long-term career mobility have produced high rates of unionisation and a fairly militant style of bargaining. The parallels with clerical work are obvious.

However, the same strong objections have to be entered against construing these developments as signalling a fundamental leftward shift in values. The 'state professions' have pursued their interests against employers in a largely instrumental fashion which eschews wider political aims of a radical kind. On balance, this can be fairly said even of middle-class unionism in France, where the links between manual and non-manual unions have given rise to a greater degree of concerted action than is found in other countries (Crozier 1962; Clark 1967).

Table 4.4 Social origins of men in 'prestigious' occupations in 1966

Type of employment	Professional and intermediate	Other non-manual	Manual	Other*	All Classes	No.
	%	%	%	%	%	
Legal profession	64	11	11	14	100	414
General management	56	9	19	15	100	618
Administrative class of the Home Civil Service	45	14	14	26	100	84
All Men	46	14	26	14	100	9404

* Including cases in which father's social class is unknown.
Source: Kelsall *et al*., 1972:214

None of the foregoing discussion, therefore, should be allowed to obscure the critical fact that the middle-class radical is a rare bird. This is true even if 'radicalism' is interpreted to mean dissenting political activism on a non-class issue like nuclear disarmament. Despite all economic and cultural cleavages

> 'it can be said, with truth and with very practical implications, that a large proportion of the heterogeneous groups that make up the middle classes have a common concern with the defence of economic and social inequality against the levelling tendencies which threaten either their incomes or their property or those parts of the social structure which narrow the ways of entry into the better

> paid occupations and thus keep down the competition for superior jobs. This when it comes to the point is their chief common interest; for the defence of culture and of the higher liberal values is the concern only of a fraction of the middle classes, and that by no means the most influential fraction when they attempt to act together as a class' (Cole 1950:288).

The striking fact is that, as Lockwood observes (1958:209), the dominant values of capitalist society are those of the entrepreneurial and professional *middle* classes, and there is little doubt that this alliance has been deliberately fostered by propertied interests. Middle-class meritocratic egalitarianism is the natural enemy of greater equality of condition, since it takes for granted the structured inequalities as a way of achieving individual mobility. On one level, noticeable divisions within the middle classes have to be acknowledged, as does the fact that their lower echelons have experienced a quite drastic deterioration of class situation. 'Support' for middle-class values may amount to no more than tacit and unreflecting acceptance of the existing social order, and conservative voting, for instance, may be simply regarded as the lesser of two evils. Still, when all due qualifications have been made, the middle classes have justified Marx's prediction of their role, that of bolstering 'the social security and power of the upper ten thousand'.

The Embourgeoisement Thesis

Arguments about the 'proletarianisation' of the less privileged strata among the middle classes have had their analogue in the 'embourgeoisement' thesis — the notion that the working class is losing its discrete social and political entity. The quality of these writings varies considerably. Zweig's work (1961), which gave an impetus to the whole debate in the British setting, still makes interesting reading, and does in fact try to deal with the underlying structural changes in the class situation of workers, which affluence merely symbolises. Nevertheless, it is a fair criticism that he infers far too much from the fact of the postwar consumer revolution. Much more questionable have been the attempts to deduce a trend towards middle-class attitudes from voting patterns (see, for example, Abrams and Rose 1960). This was a dubious procedure even on straight statistical grounds, since electoral 'swings' tend not to be very large, and no certainty existed that the working class did in fact supply the defectors from Labour. Furthermore, studies of this kind did a great deal to propagate the notion that a simplistic connection between affluence and conservatism could be taken for granted. It was largely left to the critics of the embourgeoisement idea to devise a rigorous analytical model which could reveal, not merely what might have caused such an important transformation, but whether it had occurred at all. Goldthorpe and Lockwood (1963) suggested that three related kinds of change would be detectable in a situation of 'inegalitarian classlessness'. Changes in the *class* situation of manual workers would be one such dimension of change, obviously, this understood to mean a consideration of both market and work situations. The more favourable this class situation had become over time, the more one could expect a corresponding diminution of *normative* differentiation, so that the working-class meaning-system would increasingly approximate that of the middle classes. Lastly, the breaking down of class barriers would be reflected in *relational* patterns. That is, not only would distinctively working- and middle-class styles of leisure and sociability disappear, but the classes would themselves find no obstacles to informal interaction.

These dimensions of change were subsequently put to the test in a survey of affluent car-workers in Luton (Goldthorpe *et al.* 1968, 1968a, 1969). Luton was a likely spot for the 'middle-class' worker, and had also attracted Zweig's attention. Economically a 'boom' town, it also lies at some distance from the traditional working-class communities of the heavily industrialised Midlands, which it does not resemble. The men in the sample were largely from other, distant parts of the country, and housed in new, socially and relatively heterogeneous complexes, many of them built by private developers. The firms for which they worked, in addition to paying high wages, were noted for progressive welfare and personnel policies. Yet,

> '. . . despite his affluence, the worker's experience of the social divisions of the work-place, of the power and remoteness of management, and of his own inconsiderable chances of ever being anything but a manual wage-earner, all dispose him to think of himself as a member of the class of "ordinary workers", and to seek collective rather than individualistic solutions to his problems. . . . Thus, although the division between "us" and "them" may have become less evident in terms of income and living standards, and at the same time less dominant in the worker's "image" of the social order, it is nonetheless one which still in fact persists in the relationships of both work and community life' (Goldthorpe *et al.* 1969:78-9).

Table 4.5 Median earnings, males, both races, year-round full-time workers, 1965, United States

Professionals	$8,459
Managers	7,895
Clerical	6,280
Sales Workers	7,226
Craftsmen (excluding foremen)	6,583
Semiskilled Operatives	5,782
Service Workers (excluding private household)	4,874
Unskilled Laborers (excluding farm and mine)	4,651

Source: Shostak 1969:69

As noted in the previous chapter, the claims concerning working-class affluence have been the subject of quite absurd exaggeration. In the United States, where workers have enjoyed the greatest sustained prosperity in the postwar world, the very lowest kinds of non-manual employment have maintained a broad parity of incomes. The workers in the Luton sample, far from coining it, were very much *lower* middle class in terms of their average weekly paypacket.

Furthermore, they were well aware that promotion was unlikely to bring about a drastic change in their situation. Three-quarters of the men considered that supervisory shop-floor jobs were the highest they could realistically aspire to, while more than four out of five of the lower-white-collar respondents believed that an able employee could reach the levels of at least middle management (Goldthorpe *et al*. 1969:76).

What was of particular interest was the affluent workers' pessimism about the long-term demand for their labour, despite the firm's remarkable record of stability and their own low exposure to unemployment. Less than one in five of them thought their job could be described as 'dead safe', and of the three-quarters who conceded that it was 'fairly safe', a large minority added that '*no* job is dead safe' (Goldthorpe *et al*. 1968:118). The threat of unemployment is perhaps the greatest single psychological burden of the worker. Needless to say, recessions immediately claim unskilled and semi-skilled workers as their first victims, but skilled manual work is by no means immune from lay-offs. In the main, the worker's skills are tied to a particular job in a particular industry, and very often there is no alternative work available in the locality. It misses the point, in this context, to talk about the affluence of capitalist economies – for example, in early 1961 there was an unemployment rate of 10 percent among skilled workers in the United States. Severe temporary crisis can easily overtake substantial segments of the labour force even during 'boom' periods, in the form of short-term unemployment, loss of overtime earnings, a curtailed working week, and so on. This fact feeds a deep-seated collective insecurity which has proved well founded time and again (Kolko 1962:78).

The fact of affluence necessarily *intensifies* some aspects of class differentiation associated with the work situation. The rationalisation of production, with its consequent fragmentation and speeding-up of tasks introduces important new strains and deprivations into the worker's life. Moreover, a century characterised by the extension of leisure has done relatively little to alter conditions for manual labour. In 1955

Table 4.6 Distribution of the unemployed, percent and rate, by occupation, both races, 1950-1968, United States.

	1950	1955	1960	1965	Unemployment Rate: 1965,	1968
Professionals	3.1%	2.2%	3.4%	3.8%	1.5	1.2
Managers	3.2	2.2	2.5	2.4	1.1	1.0
Clerical	8.2	8.0	9.8	10.8	3.3	3.0
Sales	4.9	3.6	4.2	4.7	3.4	2.8
Craftsmen	13.8	12.8	12.1	9.9	3.6	2.4
Operatives	26.9	28.2	26.5	22.4	5.5	4.5
Laborers	14.2	15.3	13.3	10.2	8.6	7.2
Service	10.3	11.7	9.9	11.9	5.5	4.6
Others (Farm; Private Household; No previous work experience)	15.4	16.0	18.3	23.9	2.6 (Farm only)	2.1

Source: Shostak 1969:76

workers continued to put in the equivalent of a six-day week in Britain and in 1968, at the height of the 'boom' years, their take-home pay was some 70 percent higher than the basic rates (Halsey ed. 1972). Both these facts indicate the part played by productivity in forming working-class incomes. Long hours, greater physical effort, shift work, overtime – all these impinge heavily on the availability and use of leisure, and go far towards precluding the emergence of middle-class styles of living, as Young and Willmott discovered (1960:96-7): '"By the time I come home", said a railway worker, "there's only time to have something to eat and take it easy by the TV" "I don't get time for anything like that", an electrician said. A docker explained that he was too exhausted by his heavy manual job: 'I don't know about other people, I'm too tired for all that. When I come home I've had it. It's all taken out of me".' Young and Willmott also found that middle-class voluntary associations often practised the deliberate exclusion of manual workers on status grounds. Whatever sociologists thought at the time, therefore, evidently the middle classes themselves held no brief for the embourgeoisement idea.

Political attitudes were remarkably unambiguous. It emerged that among the Luton sample support for the Labour Party was 'exceptionally strong' — stronger in fact than among the working class as a whole (Goldthorpe *et al.* 1968a:14-15). This finding was very striking, given the unusual characteristics of the Luton sample. Here, if anywhere, it should have been possible to discover the working-class 'suburbanite', merging imperceptibly into, even if not actually indistinguishable from, middle-class society. Yet party choice was only one aspect of an unmistakeably working-class culture which, whatever changes it may have undergone, showed no sign of being swallowed up in a classless society. Kin, neighbours and workmates (and their wives) formed the more or less exclusive basis for socialising; and working-class couples were quite clearly differentiated from even routine non-manual people in terms of their involvement in voluntary associations within the community. Both of these findings are entirely in accord with those in other studies (see, e.g., Jackson 1962; Bottomore 1954). In view of the earlier objections raised against occupational prestige rankings, it is worth making special mention of the respondents' attitudes regarding choice of company. Asked what kind of friends they would like to have around them, given a free choice, a majority (59 percent) answered 'people with a similar background and outlook'. A further quarter opted for 'people who are good company even if they can be a bit common at times'. Only 6 percent chose 'people with a good education' and a mere 1 percent 'people who have a bit of class about them'. No sign here of anything but a massive indifference to the status-striving sometimes said to be the leading psychological characteristic of the postwar working class.

It would be tiresome and pointless to continue multiplying empirical instances because they all confirm the same thing, that affluent workers do not behave and think in typically middle-class ways. As the previous chapter showed, affluence has in any case benefited the working class as a whole much less than popular belief would lead us to suppose. Its main effect upon the class structure has not worked through income distribution but through the full employment which has accompanied it. The more grandiose claims of embourgoisement theorists, however, will not hold water. Not only are claims concerning the transformation of the market position of manual labour much exaggerated, but the work situation rarely gets any attention at all. This is a serious omission since boredom, fatigue, noise, dirt, are commonplaces of working-class jobs, and prime sources of dissatisfaction and strain among manual labour. Sometimes Marx's vision of the worker as a dehumanised extension of the machine is a sober reality. An 18-year old girl working as a packer on a conveyor belt:

> 'I go terrible sometimes just thinking about coming to work in the mornings. It's not hard work but it seems to wear you out. When you don't talk it's terrible — it's a real drag — you could scream. Someone went like that last week. You've just got to control yourself' (Beynon and Blackburn 1972:74).

Furthermore, the physical and social segregation between staff and works imposed by the division of labour unambiguously symbolises the authority structure of the enterprise. The 'us-them' character of the working-class outlook can be understood as the ideological expression of daily experiences at the workplace, in the sense that the large-scale, bureaucratically organised work organisation reproduces in many fundamental respects a structure of social relationships homologous with those in society at large.

Blauner (1964) lays heavy stress on the diversity of industrial environments. His is an influential and highly readable account of the consequences of different types of technology for what he calls 'alienation' in work — a rather misleading term, as many have pointed out, which would really be better rendered as 'job satisfaction'. Blauner suggests that it is possible to distinguish four modes of alienation in the workplace: powerlessness, or lack of job control; the meaninglessness of a repetitive and limited task; social alienation, where the workers cannot form solidary social groupings; and self-estrangement, where the content of the job brings none of the intrinsic satisfactions of craftsmanship. He attacked the habit of using the automobile assembly-line worker as a case illustrating the nature of manual work generally, and these analytical distinctions are designed to serve the purpose of constructing a more detailed typology of work settings, based upon *technology* as the key variable.

The book is valuable in that it is one of the few written from a broadly end-of-ideologist viewpoint which deals with the working class as producers rather than consumers. It has a critical central weakness, however, which is a deficient sense of relativism. To say that some manual workers are more 'alienated' by their work than others is an unproblematical statement, and the reasons for this are interesting on their own. But to claim (Blauner 1964:182-3) a major transformation in the industrial culture of evolving capitalism is another matter. Blauner argues for something like this in terms of a contrast between assembly-line technology and continuous-process automation, as exemplified by car workers and chemical workers respectively:

> 'The social personality of the auto worker, a product of metropolitan residence and exposure to large, impersonal bureaucracies, is expressed in a characteristic attitude of cynicism toward authority and institutional systems, and a volatility revealed in aggressive responses to infringements on personal rights and occasional militant collective action. . . . In the chemical industry, on the other hand, continuous process technology and more favourable economic conditions result in a social structure with a high degree of consensus between workers and management and an integrated industrial community in which employees experience a sense of belonging and membership' (Blauner 1964:178).

In the first place one may question how far such changes in technology are likely to affect large portions of the labour force, a problem which Blauner himself sees is a tricky one. Furthermore, he overstates the degree of integration and consensus propagated by such industrial settings. Wedderburn and Crompton found that among the chemical process workers they studied there was indeed a quite highly developed sense of occupational identity, and workers had a sense of responsibility and control over the job which went some way towards ousting extrinsic rewards as the sole justification for work. Nevertheless, these workers were no less critical of management than others, just as resentful of being anonymous units in a big enterprise, similarly instrumental in their general attitudes to work (Wedderburn and Crompton 1972: 149). *Other things being equal* these workers were somewhat less disposed to industrial conflict, but the level of pay and physical conditions of work were far and away the most important considerations among all the men in their definition of a good job (Wedderburn and Crompton 1972:97).

This is just another way of saying that variations in what Blauner calls alienation occur *within* a context of broad similarities of class experience — and particularly of the labour market — which override the differentiating effects generated by the technologies appropriate to this industry or that. His entire discussion is distorted from the outset by the assumption that,

> 'The *worker*, who in classical capitalism was considered virtually a commodity or a cost of production and treated as a *thing*, is giving way to the *employee*, a permanent worker who is viewed much more as a *human being*. Many employees have job security based on seniority provisions or a "de facto" common law right to their jobs. The employment relationship no longer reflects merely the balance of power; it is more and more determined by a system of institutional justice' (Blauner 1964:19).

One can only say of this statement that it is simply not true, and no doubt it would be greeted with a collective raspberry by all those permanent workers pushed into the dole queues during the recession of the seventies. The payment of the weekly wage is a studied exercise in short-term accounting which flatly contradicts Blauner's optimistic premisses. Working-class security and bargaining power depend, first and last, on competition between employers for scarce labour.

Blauner, in fact, is only intermittently and unsystematically concerned with those out-plant influences and experiences which working-class people typically *share*, influences which are critical in explaining attitudinal variations. The evidence overwhelmingly supports the view that technological differences have a very limited, localised effect on workers' perceptions of the class order (Goldthorpe *et al.* 1968:181; Wedderburn and Crompton 1972:148). Insofar as the workers' superiors in the division of labour are technical collaborators on whom the operatives consistently depend for advice and assistance in their own work roles, their attitudes to management tend to be relatively favourable. Thus far, functional integration and social integration go together. However, the degree of social integration possible is necessarily limited, since on a more general level of action workers and management are on opposite sides in the system of collective bargaining. Moreover, beyond the factory walls workers are often bound into a subculture which is socially and politically isolated from the bosses and their representatives. (This issue is dealt with more fully in chapter 5.) Even shop-floor harmony, however, is likely to be missing when authority figures operate exclusively as overseers whose job it is to see that management gets what it considers to be value for money in terms of output. A distinction has therefore been found useful between what Giddens (1973:86) calls the paratechnical relations in the workplace, which are determined by the relationship of men to machinery and thus to each other; and the authority structure of the enterprise, which can vary independently of the constraints imposed by technology. For example, the car assembly-line operatives are in many respects ruled by the track, which simultaneously inhibits the possibility of interaction with workmates. This is in principle different from the existence of managerial rules designed to stop him wasting time chatting to friends.

To repeat, however, this distinction is primarily of interest in investigating variations in job satisfaction, and in management-worker relationships in face-to-face settings. In the present discussion, two other factors are of greater importance. Firstly, compared with the middle classes generally, the working environment of manual labour is qualitatively different, both in terms of pleasantness of conditions and intrinsic satisfactions deriving from the task. Secondly, despite *some* variations due to technological imperatives, the division of labour within the enterprise continues to overlap with the distribution of authority, thus reinforcing those other dimensions of class differentiation arising from the market. What is more, both sets of conditions are integral features of large-scale, bureaucratic work organisations. Postmen, to take an instance, are subjected to much the same sort of conditions with similar consequences, despite the fact that they work in a nationalised industry, and that one would be hard put to say just what 'technology' was involved in the job. Such work organisations rationalise and sub-divide tasks, which both increase the boredom of work and reduce the skill differentials of the labour force; they concentrate operatives in 'mass' settings; they elongate the span of control, and enforce close supervision over the work task, both of which make the authority structure 'visible' to workers; and they enforce different payment systems for workers and 'staff' in addition to discriminations in matters of fringe benefits, both of which underline the position of the former as subordinate sellers of labour-power, rather than members of the apparatus of control.

Irrespective of skill level and technology, Ingham (1970) has demonstrated very pronounced differences of attitudes between workers in small and large firms. In one sense, of course, all workers still tend to be employed in fairly 'small-scale' settings — the two large plants he studied employed 158 and 90 men. The point is, rather, that the overall size of the organisation (5,000 and 3,000 employees respectively) is related to levels of functional specialisation and bureaucratisation; a small firm being defined as one employing less than 100 people, and a large one 3,000 or more (Ingham 1970:61-5). The numerical 'break-points', Ingham himself admits, are somewhat arbitrary, but they are perfectly serviceable for indicating the orders of magnitude at which significant variations can be expected to appear. As to functional specialisation,

'it emerged that men in the small firms would take a partly

> finished product to another machine to complete the whole process rather than leave it for the next man if he were busy. Furthermore. . .job rotation of this kind was strongly encouraged by the management and the reasons for this would seem to stem from the exigencies posed by small scale. . . .The absence of a single man in the small firm could mean that a whole link in production might be broken; whereas in the large firm it is unlikely that absence in one department could be of such a scale as to cause the system to break down. Thus, it is important that small firms have labour forces with a variety of skills and a knowledge of the whole production process in order that adaptation can occur in disruptive situations of the kind described above' (Ingham 1970:77).

Statistically, the difference between the two types of organisation can be summed up in the fact that between 65 and 78 percent of workers in the large plants never moved from their own machine, compared with only one-fifth in the small firms (Ingham 1970:78). This has obvious implications not just for job satisfaction but also for greater dependence of the employer upon each of his employees individually.

High levels of bureaucratisation likewise transform the social relations of the workplace, and depend upon functional specialisation as well as expressing it. The extended division of labour found in large firms means that frequent contact with superiors is not merely impossible, but is in fact designed to obviate the need for it. Now it is not at all implied that management-worker interaction leads to social integration of itself, but it is a useful index of the extent to which work becomes de-personalised. Workers are evidently very sensitive to what they see as their treatment as mere 'hands', faceless human adjuncts to the plant. Wedderburn and Crompton (1972:39) report that 40 percent of their respondents *spontaneously* mentioned regimentation and anonymity as aspects of the work situation they disliked. Large plants also present barriers to the development of peer-group relations, although the difference between them and small firms in this respect is less marked (Ingham 1970:100). Again, the critical factor would seem to be not technological but social. The organisation of work in large plants is such that there is a continuous flow of jobs, leaving no natural breaks between the completion of one task and the next. What large plants do offer, of course, is higher incomes, but not all workers find this sufficient compensation for submitting themselves to the impersonal constraints of a highly rationalised productive system. Workers in small firms were just as likely to be satisfied with their incomes as those in large concerns, despite the substantially higher wages of the latter. Almost to a man, moreover, they mentioned the non-economic rewards of working as the thing they liked best in their present job, something which figured very little in the responses of the men in big plants (Ingham 1970:106-7). The contrast here, as Ingham constantly reiterates, is not between 'happy' workers and 'alienated' ones. For example, between 37 and 50 percent of *all* the men were dissatisfied with their incomes, and workers in small firms do not go to work because it is a fun thing to do. What the study does show is that the authority structure of the enterprise can be experienced with varying degrees of immediacy and antagonism. Whereas men in small firms were very likely to have, and to value, friendly personalised relations with the foreman, those in the large plants — and especially the semi-skilled men — defined a 'good' relationship with him as one where he 'leaves us alone' or 'we never see him' (Ingham 1970:103).

Although it is reasonable to talk about these attitudinal variations in terms of their congruence with class consciousness, how industrial attitudes are shaped and channelled into political behaviour must remain a separate question. Large plants have long been observed as structural features of industrial organisation associated with higher than average 'leftist' voting among workers (cf. Kerr and Siegel 1954; Lipset 1975). This problem is dealt with by Ingham (1969) in a separate paper. As a preliminary, it must be emphasised once more that plant size is only *one* factor linked with political behaviour. Thus, Ingham found that in the small firms 62 percent of workers voted Labour, the same proportion as in one of the large plants. The relevant contrast here is with the work of Stacey (1960). Her work in Banbury suggests that where a 'traditional', paternalistic relationship at work is overlaid by an essentially similar set of social relationships within a small, stable local community, it provides a total environment in which class differentiation is to a considerable degree supplanted by an integrated status order (see also Plowman *et al.* 1962). Workers in the 'traditional' firms, unlike those in the newer (and bigger) ones which had recently come into the district, were strongly Conservative in their political alignments. Since all Ingham's enterprises were located in the city of Bradford, it came as no surprise that the level of Labour voting among all his respondents was no different than for the working class as a whole. Nonetheless, he did feel able to claim quite unambiguous ideological cleavages within the sample. On the most immediate level, about three-quarters of the men in small firms agreed that 'trade unions have too much power', while in the two large plants the same percentage disagreed. However, a straight party-choice dichotomy conceals other important differences between the two settings. Small-firm Conservatives were hostile to the specifically socialist aspects of Labour policy, such as the commitment to nationalisation; their co-voters in large plants gave 'non-ideological' reasons for their choice, stressing the better economic performance of the Conservative party. Similarly, Labour voters in the large plants were more left-wing than their counterparts in small firms. Within the ideological limits implied by this discussion, therefore, large plants encourage the diffusion of class-conscious attitudes, and have an independent influence on political behaviour (Ingham 1969:243-5).

The link between the work situation and wider political processes is obviously a complex one, and for this reason it is useful to consider large and small enterprises as constituting two somewhat distinctive social systems created by the cumulative operation of a multiplicity of influences. The rationalising intentions underlying large-scale production themselves go a long way toward explaining the emergence of collective opposition to managements. The control system of a small firm is largely informally maintained, in contrast to the rather more repressive rules typically promulgated in mass settings, where workers often combine to exercise some degree of *de facto* control of the shop floor. Continuous mass production also leads to the finest calculation of job rates, and generates various strategies designed to regulate the pace of work in relation to payment. When the estimator comes round to time a new task, the chosen operative is likely to 'go by the book' and take his time. In the same way, work groups frequently take steps to restrict effort, so as not to spoil a 'gravy' job by maintaining productivity at a rate which causes management to re-time it. Furthermore, the relationship between a specialised task and the entire productive process is invisible, and any interruption in the flow of work at once leads to criticism and suspicion of management. In the small firm, such problems are immediately intelligible and interpreted as a shared difficulty requiring a cooperative solution. Small concerns are also unlikely to have the social and physical segregation which the mass-production system enforces. Relations with owners and managers are characterised by a friendly paternalism, and these figures of course have nothing in common except the title with their counter-parts in the powerful corporate enterprises. Small firms have little in the way of 'middle' management, and no army of administrators at the routine white-collar level, enjoying their quasi-managerial perks and privileges. Manual workers, Lockwood suggests, frequently see this group as 'pen-pushers' and 'guvnor's men', and it is thus highly likely that such people, on a mundane, day-to-day basis, exert a strong influence on working-class perceptions of authority. Lastly, it is essential not to miss the point that class attitudes are informed by objective assessments of the situation, which structure norms according to a rational strategy for action. Lupton (1963) has shown how, in a garment factory, a strong instrumental cooperation with management developed in response to the need to compete in a very tight market, and it is all too easily forgotten that workers are perfectly capable of forming accurate judgments of this kind. Small firms often exist uneasily in the shadow of giant, monopolistic combines, sometimes in competition with other small firms, specialising in short 'uneconomic' runs or items for which mass-production techniques are unsuitable. Work and market situation meet at this point, so to speak, and give point to Worsley's observation (1964:25-6) that sociological investigation is most fertile when directed to the interplay of 'subjective' and 'objective' influences on social action. Class consciousness does not develop through a process of ratiocination, but through the experience of concrete situations in which the means of collective action — organisation — are developed to pursue given ends.

This does *not* mean, of course, that the translation of the forms of collective opposition and conflict characteristic of large plants into specifically political idiom can be understood without reference to the mobilising influence of working-class organisations. The French working class, for example, has unusually high levels of class consciousness, to some extent at least because the large plants in the developed regions are dominated by the Communist-led trade unions (Hamilton 1967:275). Even the ideologically moderate trade unions however, such as are found in the United States and Britain, contribute to the strengthening of class identity. Unionism in large plants tends to be strong, partly because employers want it so — although of course they have very definite views about the legitimate political role of unions. It is only a superficial paradox that employers are often disposed to abet the extension and centralisation of trade-union organisation, since unions are key mechanisms of bureaucratic negotiation and control which have enabled capitalism to take on its most characteristic, planned corporate form. They are useful as a means of regulating a massed and potentially hostile labour force. However, the necessary price of cooperation is the acknowledgement of conflicts of interest and the acceptance of collective bargaining procedures. The 'us-them' mentality becomes embodied in an institution linked to the wider labour movement, mediated through union activists, such as shop stewards, who act as leaders of public opinion because of the part they play in dealings with management. Interestingly, workers of a militant disposition apparently find it hard to fit into the social system of the small firm (Ingham 1970:119), and unquestionably a process of self-selection occurs which reinforces the distinctive collective sentiments found in the two settings. Thus, the 'deferential' working-class Conservative is likely to value and seek the personal, friendly relations with management *and* the freedom from union influences which the small firm offers. This draws attention to the general observation that workers are not subjected to processes of political socialisation in any passive and automatic way. Individuals in large plants may bring to the work situation attitudes which are 'deviant' in terms of the dominant subculture of the enterprise, by reason of the community or biographical influences to which they are exposed. The tendency towards the preservation of middle-class values in the face of downward occupational mobility is an important instance of this. Wilensky and Edwards (1958) indicate that such 'skidders' commonly interpret their situation as a temporary one brought about by bad luck, and resist the acculturating pressures of the working-class environment. In the same way, Jackson and Marsden (1963) speak of the 'sunken middle class'. However, this brings up a set of new problems which are the concern of the final chapter.

The Aristocracy of Labour

Finally, mention must be made of the skilled, apprentice-trained craftsmen who in some respects are the 'mirror image' within the working class of the routine white-collar stratum. Skilled workers are most likely to have relatively high aspirations for their children, and account for the major part of mobility into non-manual occupations. They themselves, for obvious reasons, are the people most likely to experience career mobility into the ranks of foreman and supervisory staff. Patterns of intermarriage further testify to the relative 'looseness' of the class structure at its middle levels — a particularly common occurrence is to find skilled men with wives employed in clerical work. House-ownership is more within the reach of skilled labour, because of its favoured market situation. On the other hand, they share with their less skilled colleagues a broadly similar work situation, in addition to the fact that their market chances can by no means said to have been assimilated to those of the lower-middle-class overall. Skilled work, nevertheless does have some claim to be considered as a source of horizontal differentiation within the manual ranks in a way which invites obvious comparisons with clerical labour.

Mackenzie's study (1973) of American craftsmen suggests the view that changes in the class situation of clerical labour have been far more important than any process of embourgeoisement among manual workers. Although both groups, for example, identify themselves as members of a 'middle mass' of occupations set apart both from labour as a whole and from the established middle classes, it is noticeable that there has not been any comparable process of social homogenisation in relational patterns among them. Furthermore, in certain important respects the craftsmen do continue to attach considerable importance to what might be termed the non-manual barrier. They were asked to choose a job for a son, if the alternatives were between him becoming a plumber at $150 a week and a bookkeeper at $120 a week; 37 percent of them gave the first answer and 47 percent the second. Given that these men were very much members of a 'labour aristocracy', what is remarkable is not that four out of ten chose the 'plumber' option — a job very like their own — but that more did not do so. Two sorts of reasoning were paramount in their explanations. Two-thirds of the craftsmen stressed the long-term possibilities for upward mobility, giving responses like: 'Not a labouring job. It's white collar. You can better yourself by staying away from labour — eventually he would progress more. In the long run it would pay off'. Also very salient in the minds of the group were what they considered to be very negative aspects of their working conditions. As one electrician expressed the matter, 'the body can only take so much' (Mackenzie 1973:61ff). The fact that these attitudes persist among the most privileged workers in the United States is impressive. Its powerful postwar economy has given the working class a degree of affluence and security unmatched anywhere else, and there is a notable absence of ideological influences which stress the status superiority of non-manual employment. The weakening of middle-class attitudes among clerical labour is a much more striking feature of the study. The United States' occupational structure has gone far beyond any other in proliferating this kind of work. Half the workforce is employed in non-manual occupations, a high proportion of it in lowly capacities; not clerical workers only, but salespeople and the motley array of occupations needed to run a service-oriented, high-consumption economy. It is here that one should look for the most dramatic changes at the middle levels of the class structure.

Historically, the justification for treating the 'aristocracy of labour' as a separate and homogeneous stratum is very much stronger than at the present time. The term itself was coined by an historian (see Hobsbawm 1967), and is not to be transferred indiscriminately to the 'skilled' working class. Gray's work (1974), for example, on the artisans of Victorian Edinburgh, leaves no doubt that the economic and social differentiation between them and the mass of the (largely unskilled) working class far outstripped any contrasts between manual and non-manual labour. This distinctive position within the class structure was reflected and reinforced by the early and separate development of craft unionism, which has been a powerful source of internal division within many labour movements, and particularly in the United States (Mackenzie 1973:173). This exclusiveness has been broken down from two directions. The less skilled workers have themselves become organised and unionised, partly through the example and leadership of craftsmen; and they typically need a modicum (it is rarely more than a few weeks) of on-the-job training before they can be of use to an employer. On both counts, their class situation has significantly altered from the days when manual labour, for a mass of workers, meant essentially *casual* employment. On the other hand, there is little reason to doubt that the emergence of large-scale enterprise has worked to reduce the social and political isolationism of the 'natural' leaders of labour. Skilled men nowadays are chiefly found as a segment of the workforce within a big concern, and to some extent at least a common employer gives rise to common interests and problems. Perhaps more significant is the tendency of rationalised production to break down the complexity and market value of craft skills — indeed to obliterate many of them altogether. The 'skilled' designation must be understood in a relative sense, comparing it with the overall character of manual work. Recent research has shown that,

> 'out of over 350 different jobs across one labour market, only a very few allow the worker to exercise as much intrinsic job skill as he would use if driving to work' (Mann 1973:25).

There are many signs of this process of change in the situation of skilled men. It is a universal complaint among craftsmen that they have no opportunity to use their training, to 'do a good job'. Career mobility on the technical side is becoming increasingly hard to achieve, owing to the emphasis on formal qualifications, in contrast to the days when between the 'mechanic' and the 'engineer' no very hard and fast line could be drawn. The role of foreman too has undergone quite unambivalent changes in the direction of functional specialisation and simplification. Where once he discharged quasi-managerial duties — such as hiring and firing work gangs — he is nowadays only the last link in an extended, bureaucratised chain of command (Bendix 1963:213).

All the evidence goes to confirm the view that skilled workers are only *marginally* differentiated from the rest. Wedderburn and Crompton (1972:143-4) argue for a distinction between 'craft' and 'class' consciousness, on the grounds that craft militancy is based on a more conservative, status-conscious structure of values. But their own findings constantly contradict this distinction. There was a group of militant craftsmen on the site who 'regarded the general workers as "Carnation Milk" creatures, as one shop steward put it. By this he meant that, by his standards, they were docile and easily persuaded by management' (Wedderburn and Crompton 1972:141).

There could obviously, therefore, be no simple division between the class-conscious general workers and the craftsmen. Moreover, as a *group* the craftsmen were fractionally more likely to reject the cooperative, 'football team' analogy of worker-management relations than two out the three groups of general workers studied (Wedderburn and Crompton 1972:43). They were also markedly more critical of pay relativities than general workers; nearly three-quarters judged the white-collar and supervisory grades to be overpaid. Furthermore, they were conscious not only of their own relative deprivation, but had a wider frame of reference which included other groups of workers:

> 'it was the tradesmen who thought that significant groups of the general workers were underpaid. In reply to the question "Are there any groups of workers here who you think get paid too little for what they do" a quarter said 'tradesmen', but another quarter named process workers, 19 percent tradesmen's mates, and 32 percent the general labourers, i.e., the lowest paid of the unskilled workers' (Wedderburn and Crompton 1972:106).

It is *not* legitimate to offer as evidence of class consciousness the more overtly hostile, but (understandably) extremely narrowly-framed responses of a section of the general workers to the question whether management and workers were on the 'same' or 'opposite' sides of industry. On the contrary, while the general workers gave answers like 'teamwork's a load of rubbish', it was a minority of the *craftsmen* who said things like, 'The capitalists are on one side of the fence and we're on the other' (Wedderburn and Crompton 1972:44-5), thereby actually transposing the terms of the original question into politicised form. Even where it is not radically expressed, the outlook of these craftsmen could be argued to be closer to the attitudes implied by consciousness of *class* than that of the general workers.

In a general way, the case for singling out skilled workers as a differentiated stratum within the ranks of manual labour is a weak one, whatever the validity of the concept of a labour aristocracy for the analysis of nineteenth-century class structure. Far from experiencing a process of partial extrusion from the working class, skilled labour has lost ground relative to other groups of workers. The assumption, therefore, that the 'upper' ranks of manual workers — whether defined by affluence, skills, or any other criterion — must show a normative shift in the direction of 'middle-classness' is even less likely to be true than the corresponding argument for clerical labour. And a plethora of attitudinal surveys reveal an essential homogeneity of outlook between skill levels in any given study — towards management, towards the job, towards trade unionism, or whatever. The influence of large- and small-scale organisation on workers' attitudes indicates very clearly that variations in class consciousness are more plausibly related to differences which affect whole groups of workers than to individual skills. At the same time, it *is* the skilled stratum which, as just noted, accounts for most upward mobility into the middle classes, is more likely to vote Conservative, and so on. There is an obvious paradox here.

The solution to this paradox lies in the fact that the skilled stratum is itself split. The Luton researchers, for example, found that skilled workers supplied a high proportion of activists in unions, and are much more likely to join unions out of principle than for the selective benefits membership confers. This may itself express only trade-union consciousness (as the authors claim), but it still distinguishes skilled workers as a group from their fellows. Attitudinal variations among *all* workers, on the other hand, are most closely related to the extent that individuals have parental and conjugal connections with the middle class. Thus, it was the workers who had no such links with the middle class who were most resentful of the fact that management and workers had separate eating facilities; and these workers again who provided the solid backbone of support for the Labour Party (Goldthorpe *et al.* 1969: 175, table 22;71 table 5). There is of course an empirical correlation between these variations and skill levels, because the skilled stratum is the 'receiving group' for most of what downward mobility and social mixing takes place. Nevertheless, it is a mistake to look for a causal explanation in the intrinsic features of the class situation of skilled labour, because what is at issue is the diffusion of middle-class normative influences within the working class *as a whole*. Upward mobility too is, predictably, heavily conditioned by such influences. One American study showed that children with middle-class mothers were about twice as likely to go to college as those born to working-class women (Parkin 1972:56) — the phenomenon of the 'sunken middle class' again. There is no reason why skilled workers should be less susceptible than others to working-class values, given that most of them are exposed to no others on the crucial level of interpersonal socialisation.

Class Structuration and Meaning-System

In general terms, this chapter has argued, levels of class awareness and identification depend upon two sets of conditions:

1. Variations in the market and work situations of different groups, which predispose them to 'us-them' images of society on the one hand, or to 'prestige' images on the other.
2. The degree of social closure any group experiences, this being reflected in mobility chances.

Together, they define what Giddens (1973:107-12) calls class structuration. It is a mistake, he argues, to see a complex phenomenon in terms of simple class 'boundaries'. Only in the case where the sources of class structuration are mutually reinforcing in their operation could we expect the development of something approximating to the ideal-typical class perspectives outlined at the beginning of the chapter.

This approach to the problem of class differentiation is an extremely flexible and useful one. Although it has proved of very great value in explaining why an important line of division separates the working and middle classes, it is not *theoretically* limited to this question. On the contrary, the notion of class structuration can be used in principle to account for multiple cleavages based on the division of labour, and the way in which they change through time. Both Lockwood and Mackenzie do just this, by suggesting that another, though at present very much secondary, point of social differentiation has appeared *within* the middle classes as now conventionally termed. From another angle, the analysis of variations in degrees of class structuration can be used equally well as a way of explaining variations in the meaning-system of the working class, both in time and place. And this in turn provides a point of entry into the discussion of the related, though analytically distinct, problems of class consciousness and class conflict.

5 Proletarians, privatisation and parties

While the conditions and rewards of manual labour may be an endemic source of tension and dissatisfaction in the minds of disprivileged individuals, class consciousness is something else again. A central theme of the previous chapter was that working-class collectivism cannot be taken for granted as a 'natural' response to market inequalities. The workplace is critical in providing the social setting (or 'material base', in Marx's terminology) within which solidarism and opposition to capitalist institutions have their origins. However, it would be very surprising if working-class consciousness were uniform in time and place, given the diversity of conditions which capitalist societies provide. The problem, therefore, is to develop a typology of social settings which make for class-conscious organisation and action, and thus explain observed variations of attitudes among the working class.

The concept of 'occupational community' is helpful here. Jobs which are dangerous, or require physical toughness, or demand close team-work often unite the workers in an industry — fishermen, miners and steelworkers are instances where all three conditions run together, and all three of these groups of workers are marked by a strong sense of their occupational identity. Isolation, either on the basis of geography or peculiar hours of work, may also bring about the same effect: truck drivers and railwaymen are pertinent examples. Clearly, when both sets of conditions apply, as in the case of fishermen and miners, one would expect to find a very high degree of solidarism among workers (see, on all this, Blauner 1966). Kerr and Siegel (1954) discovered among spatially isolated, single-class communities of workers a strong propensity to strike action. They further suggested that such strikes had the character of a 'small-scale revolt' against society, rather than of bargaining tactics designed to win specific and limited concessions from their employers. It is among groups like miners, Lockwood concludes, that we should look for the 'proletarian traditionalists' among the working class (Lockwood 1966:250). Such workers are especially predisposed to a 'power' model of society, expressed in social imagery dominated by a fundamental division between 'us' and 'them', generated by the double solidarism of work and community life.

In the making of the 'deferential traditionalist', Lockwood suggests, a quite different set of structural conditions will be decisive. The work situation of the deferential traditionalist is likely to bring him into frequent personalised contact with middle-class superiors, most often in small firms. Such a working environment is best suited to a diffuse paternalism, in which the worker is not treated purely as a source of labour. The deferential traditionalist will be supported in his social attitudes to the extent that his non-work environment mirrors his work-place relationships. It is here, if anywhere, that one can speak of a unified status order.

> 'Small, relatively isolated and economically autonomous communities, particularly those with a well-differentiated occupational structure and stable populations provide the most favourable setting for the existence of "local status systems". The key characteristic of such systems is that the allocation of status takes place through "interactional" rather than through "attributional" mechanisms. Through close acquaintance, people have a detailed knowledge of each other's personal qualities and can apply relatively complex criteria in deciding who is worthy of membership of a particular status group. There is also widespread

consensus about the rank order of status groups in the community, so that the lower strata regard their lowly position less as an injustice than as a necessary, acceptable and even desirable part in a natural system of inequality' (Lockwood 1966:254).

Despite their very different images of society, both types of traditionalist have in common an experience of the class structure which is well defined, well understood, and reinforced by the day-to-day interactions of work and leisure. As against them, Lockwood speculates that the spread of newer industries and their attendant urban growth will increasingly create a third ideal-typical individual, the privatised worker. This is partly a consequence of the technology of the newer industries which have come to dominate the contemporary capitalist economies, but it is also partly a function of the growth of anonymous urban and suburban estates which house a collection of strangers (Lockwood 1966: 257). Though segregation by class may persist, this geographical and residential mobility is held to represent a critical fracture in the patterns of sociability found in the traditional working-class community (see, for example, Hoggart 1958; Young and Willmott 1972). The removal of young families to a distance of even a few miles is sufficient to disrupt the life of the extended family centred on one or other (or both) set of in-laws. For the menfolk, work ceases to be a place where friendship and social attachments are formed, and they too are likely to live in scattered locations, making leisure-time contacts more difficult. The privatised worker thus becomes personally isolated, engrossed by home and the preoccupations of his immediate family. The experiential links between him and wider collectivities lose their binding force, and the claims of class and community loyalties are abandoned and recede. His life is reflected ideologically in a pecuniary image of society. Increasingly the privatised worker seeks exclusively money and possessions for himself, and money is the yardstick by which he measures the social standing of others.

It must be strongly emphasised that these three working-class figures continue to be hypothetical to a large extent. However, they have an obvious use in the historical investigation of variations in working-class consciousness, and were so used in the affluent-worker study. The Luton researchers demolished the embourgeoisement thesis without any difficulty, but, Mackenzie points out (1974:247), in its most simplistic form. The more difficult and interesting part of their work revolves around the evaluation of the claim, originally proposed as a possibility by Goldthorpe and Lockwood (1963), that some degree of normative convergence had taken place at the middle levels of the British class structure. In the event, the later empirical study of affluent workers was judged by its authors to vindicate the claim of a shift in the character of working-class consciousness traceable to the breaking up of the traditional proletarian community. That is to say, they came to the conclusion that the affluent workers they studied displayed attitudes which came closer to the 'privatised' worker as an ideal type than to the 'proletarian traditionalist'. Central to the outlook of the privatised worker, the authors suggest (1968:38-9), is an instrumental attitude to work which can be summed up under the following heads:

1. Work serves the purely extrinsic purpose of supporting a valued non-work existence.
2. The worker's relationship to the organisation is calculative.
3. Work is not, and is not expected to be, personally satisfying.
4. Neither the firm nor the union 'spills over' into non-work hours, in the form of commitment to solidary social groupings.

Though far from the deferential traditionalist, this 'new' working-class figure is also somewhat removed from the claustrophobic allegiances of the close-knit working-class community. Lacking affectual bonds both in and out of work, it is supposed that 'solidaristic collectivism' will give way to 'what we would call an "instrumental" orientation — to work, trade unionism and politics alike' (Goldthorpe *et al.* 1968a: 76).

This immediately raises a prickly problem as to exactly

what meaning is to be attached to the term 'instrumental'. The authors speak in another place of the 'limited, affectively neutral' nature of the worker's involvement with the job (1968: 175). Quite clearly, this points to a radical split between work and non-work, the implication being that the worker 'blanks out' the forty-odd hours he spends each week on the shop floor. In effect, then, the affluent worker is seen as a self-conscious money seeker, a model which is not far from end-of-ideologism in some ways. The situation is altogether peculiar, because the division of labour is made to lose its theoretical salience in favour of explanations in terms of workers' prior orientations to the job. Such a dichotomy was not originally proposed. That is to say, the *total* class situation was taken as relevant to explaining the non-embourgeoisement of the affluent worker, but is abandoned in the contrast between the 'traditional' and 'new' working class. Nor, as a matter of fact, did this contrast get seriously argued on an empirical level. No systematic attempt was made to weigh the attitudes of affluent workers against those to be found in more traditional industries, even though everything turns on the comparison. The 'proletarian traditionalist' remains an obdurately ideal-typical construction for the most part, and as a result there is no baseline against which to judge the alleged 'deviation' of the privatised individual from his more class-conscious peers. For example, on the question of unionism Goldthorpe and his colleagues state (1968:107):

> 'If, on the basis of evidence so far presented, we seek to make comparisons between our affluent workers and workers of a more traditional kind, the main differences, it would then seem, must be looked for not so much in the actual *degree* of participation in union affairs, but rather in the form which this takes and still more perhaps in the *meaning* which union activity appears to have for the majority of the men in question.'

But since this difference is imputed, not demonstrated, the whole very important issue is stranded on the level of hypothesis.

This fundamental lack of evidential constraint on the kinds

of interpretation which could be legitimately placed on the responses of the affluent-worker sample led inevitably to a whole gamut of questionable inferences. The discussion of unionism again provides an instance of this. The Luton team put a great many questions about the societal role of unions, but always in such a way as to elicit their workers' *perceptions* rather than their *feelings* about unionism and the working class. This is a curious omission in a study behind which stands a contrast with the 'gut' solidarism of the traditional worker. Beynon and Blackburn have shown on just this question that it is essential to distinguish sharply between what might be called practical and ethical judgments in attitudinal studies. They found that much which might be interpreted as a general indifference to the trade union movement in fact boiled down to specific grievances about union activity. As one woman put it,

> 'I didn't mind joining at the Co-op. It was a strong union there; it does something for you. Here they back down when management look at them. I'd begrudge paying my half a crown a week to this lot' (Beynon and Blackburn 1972: 121).

Some of the difficulties involved in tapping attitudes through surveys are illustrated by the fact that in Blackburn and Beynon's sample 76 percent of non-unionists thought that all workers ought to belong to one, not far short of the 86 percent of union members who agreed with their view. Now, this research was carried out in a setting very different from that of Luton, and it is *not* implied that one can assume that a similar finding would have emerged there. But due attention to the attitudes of traditional workers might well have prompted a more critical approach to the claims made for the data in the Luton study. Sometimes these claims get definitely out of hand. When asked whether trade unions should try to get workers a say in management, or confine themselves to pay and conditions, 40 percent of the men gave the first answer and 52 percent the second. Whatever the views of traditional workers on this, the figures hardly justify the bald conclusion that 'there is no very widespread desire among these men that their unions should strive to give them a share in the running of the plant' (Goldthorpe *et al.* 1968: 109).

There are other tensions in the accumulated responses to various questions which the authors freely acknowledge but do not altogether resolve. For instance, low-key union activity does not correspond to any faith in the benevolence of management. Work-study men were suspiciously regarded, by a majority of the workforce, as seeking chiefly to extract more effort from them. Similarly, all groups bar one (which divided on the question) were heavily in favour of the view that the firm could well afford to pay them more without endangering future business prospects (Goldthorpe *et al.* 1968;85-7). This is at least as consistent with a feeling of exploitation as with the assumption that it reflects a purely instrumental concern with more money. Further confusions arise in the relationship between unionism and political processes. Of the Luton sample 41 percent agreed that the trade unions have too much power in Britain, but Parkin (1972:93) reports two surveys in each of which the proportion was two-thirds. Slightly more than a half of affluent workers were opposed to trade union involvement with the Labour Party and only 46 percent of them voluntarily (as opposed to unknowingly) paid the optional political levy (Goldthorpe *et al.* 1968:110-1). Yet support for the Labour Party was 'exceptionally strong', and nearly 60 percent of the men gave specifically *class* loyalties as the reason for their support (Goldthorpe *et al.* 1968a:15-17). Once again, however, we are required to understand these responses as really expressing instrumental attitudes once more, because they 'did not mean that politics were widely represented as a manifestation of the class struggle' (Goldthorpe *et al.* 1969: 177; cf. 1968a:18-19). But where is the proletarian traditionalist who sees (or has seen) politics in this way? Presumably he is an *historical* figure since we are told that (1968a:19), 'the grounds for the high left-wing voting in our sample of affluent workers are not markedly different from those of the working class generally.' But just to confuse us still more, we learn (1968:177) of 'the *fatalistic* social philosophy which was frequently encountered among the inhabitants of the traditional working-class community' (italics added).

Reading through the affluent worker volumes, it becomes increasingly obvious not only that the traditional worker is an extremely elusive figure, but that his 'demise' tends to be accounted for more and more with reference to the physical dispersal of workers from the traditional community (1968: 174-5;1968a:74-5). In other words, what in Lockwood's (1966) essay is treated as an additional and reinforcing aspect of class. structuration comes increasingly to occupy the central place. Combined with this emphasis at the expense of the market and work situation of the affluent worker is the assertion — for it is no more — that,

> 'In consequence of the conjugal family assuming a more "companiate" or partnership-like form, relations both between husband and wife and between parents and children would seem likely to become closer and more inherently rewarding; certainly more so than could generally have been the case under the economic and social conditions of the traditional working-class community' (Goldthorpe *et al.* 1968:175).

In the absence of any definite evidence once more, one does not have to be overly cynical to suggest that the conjugal family may not be the consolation implied here. It is by no means clear that mum and the kids (plus the telly) will in most cases compensate for frustrating and boring employment, and the situation of the non-working wife would seem even less enviable. It is true that we must not 'romanticise' the life of the working-class community, but neither should we exaggerate its brutality and drunkenness at the expense of the affectual bonds on which the Luton team themselves insist so much. Like any other change, the prosaic truth is no doubt that it has both good and bad sides.

Many of the contradictions of the Luton study are concentrated in the three case studies sketched out in the first volume (1968:168-73) of Mr Doyle, Mr Taylor and Mr Grant. All three of them dislike their jobs. Work is variously described as 'irksome', 'boring and irritating', 'stressful both physically and psychologically'. Mr Grant and Mr Doyle, certainly, find nearly all their social relationships within the conjugal family, but then the working class generally do not easily create middle-class patterns of sociability (Lockwood 1966:257). This does not tell us anything positive about the compensatory functions of life at home. Only Mr Doyle definitely looks forward to staying in Luton and using his prosperity to build a better life for his family in the future. Mr Grant rather regrets his abandoned career in the merchant navy, but is partially consoled by the thought of steady and rising affluence. Mr Taylor and his wife definitely miss 'home', which means their middle-class suburb of origin and the friends they had there. True enough, all of them were attracted to Luton by security, high incomes and the prospect of finding a house — in the case of two of them it was impending marriage which precipitated the move. In one sense, therefore, it was an instrumental decision. But there is no compelling theoretical or practical reason for viewing their initial orientation to this work as permanently overriding their subsequent experiences. On the contrary, given the highly unusual character of the Luton respondents, what is truly remarkable is the rapidity with which they had been welded into a self-conscious collectivity. Nearly three-quarters of them had come from outside the Luton area, and 30 percent had experienced downward mobility from white-collar jobs. They were, in fact,

> 'in some degree "self-selected" for a high level of motivation towards material advancement. . . . found together at Luton *because* of a decision on their part to leave a former area of residence in quest of improvement, in one way or another, of their living standards' (Goldthorpe *et al.* 1968: 154).

However, the researchers contrast 'solidaristic' and 'instrumental' collectivism, and are definite that privatisation does not spell a long-term decline in collectivism as a mode of social action. It is the ends, not the means, which have changed.

The proposition is that collectivism among affluent workers serves only a mass of private interests, and is no longer linked with the more radical aims espoused by the labour movement. This is a very reasonable case to argue. Collectivism is far from being a monopoly of the working class. Professionals, in the sense earlier discussed, are the most highly organised occupational groups of all. The way in which the case in fact develops, however, is odd. The nub of the matter can perhaps be best brought out by the following remarks on the relationship between privatisation, unionism and Labour voting:

> 'Given that there are compelling reasons why affluent workers should use collective means to obtain their private ends, this does not, of course, imply that they will automatically be supporters of the Labour Party — although we can say, at the very least, that there is nothing incompatible between the two. Nevertheless, it is quite conceivable that a worker might feel that his personal economic interest could best be served by joining a trade union *and* by voting for the Conservative or Liberal Party. But again, as a matter of fact, we know from a number of studies that workers are much more likely to vote for the Labour Party if they are trade union members; and since we have already argued that there are good reasons for believing that the majority of new and affluent workers will be strongly inclined to join trade unions, then we can assume that the practice, if not the logic, of privatised self-interest will normally result in a relatively high Labour vote among the new and affluent working class' (Goldthorpe *et al.* 1968a:78).

This train of reasoning can only be termed strange, quite apart from the fact that it does not explain anything. There are many problems awaiting solution in sociology, but the relationship between trade-unionism and Labour allegiances does not appear to be one of the more urgent ones. If a worker can see that his interests can be best served by joining a trade union, the same logic (very often) will lead him to vote for the Labour Party. In political sociology the emphasis on values is important, but it should not be allowed to expunge consideration of the rational, calculative element in political behaviour. Since the unions and the Labour Party go to a great deal of trouble to explain the appeal of their organisations to working-class people, and their connections with each other, the links between the three are readily understood. In any case, the whole argument is quite superfluous, since Goldthorpe *et al.* hold that the leaders of the labour movement no longer articulate, as they once did, the radical aims necessary to bring about important changes. Labour voting, in this social context, would be completely consistent with instrumental collectivism as a constellation of values.

The fact is, however, that the Luton team totally ignore the specifically political aspects of social organisation in relation to working-class consciousness. The final volume of their study acknowledges the role played by the Labour Party in political mobilisation, but only in the form of a straightforward assertion about its declining influence. Their overriding concern with the privatisation thesis leads to a much greater stress on a contradictory postulate. The change from 'ethical' to 'business' unionism is unequivocally described as the result of 'highly functional adaptations to the changing work situation and to the changing wants and expectations of industrial employees' (Goldthorpe *et al.* 1969:170). It is hard to see how both theoretical positions can be occupied simultaneously. If union activity largely reflects members' wants and interests, *ex hypothesi* it follows that support for wider class aims will not be forthcoming. If, on the other hand, such a possibility exists, then the whole argument from 'economism' and 'instrumental collectivism' collapses. In the end, the least satisfactory exit from the deadlock is chosen. Affluent workers are credited with *suppressed* deprivations, exactly the sort of untestable supposition to which the authors object in the work of certain neo-marxist theorists (Goldthorpe *et. al.* 1969:189).

Least of all is it possible to find convincing arguments in support of the suggestion that these affluent workers can be regarded as 'prototypical' of the working class of the future (Goldthorpe *et al.* 1968:175). Putting it simply, how many repetitions of the Luton situation are we likely to see? The remarkably unchanging pattern of income distribution in capitalist societies makes it highly unlikely that the opportunity to 'exchange' high wages for stressful work and a family-centred existence would ever be possible for more than a minority. Moreover, the very conditions that made Luton a good setting in which to examine the embourgeoisement thesis made it a correspondingly bad one in which to argue for the loss of 'community' as a permanent feature of changing patterns of urban growth and technological organisation. In the words of Cousins and Davis (1974:276), 'new' workers become 'old'.

In essence, the central criticism being advanced is that the 'traditional' worker displays far too much of a tendency to appear in the guise of a *deus ex machina*, whose function it is to validate a prepared theoretical position. In moving from the ideal-typical to the historical levels of analysis, there occurs a corresponding tendency to treat as reality relationships which were previously only hypothesised, or presented in a somewhat tentative way. It should be emphasised very strongly at this point that the criticisms of the affluent-worker study just rehearsed in no way detract from its achievements. It is a very fine attempt to bridge the gap in class theory between limited empiricism and the distinctly unsatisfactory catch-all evolutionary schemes of the kind which depend for their appeal largely on an absence of data. Even less should it be supposed that the ideal-typical scheme proposed by Lockwood in his 1966 essay has been discredited. On the contrary, it has proved of remarkable analytical value.

Nevertheless, Lockwood himself has more than once acknowledged the slipperiness of the notion of 'community', and its related concepts, and Westergaard long ago framed a puzzle which has not been altogether satisfactorily resolved. He asked, simply, how the parochialism of the local community could be reconciled with the universalistic loyalties of class consciousness (Westergaard 1965:107; and 1975:*passim*). The same question has also been put by Allcorn and Marsh (1975:211) in effect, when they suggest that an explicit distinction is needed, and not always made, between the notions of solidarity and sociability. For it is patently the case that solidarity must rest on some kind of identification with wider social groupings than sociability networks can possibly represent, at least as the term solidarity is usually employed in sociological theory. (It is not legitimate to deduce from the fact that the Luton workers did not form close friendships with their working acquaintances that there was a lack of solidarity with those whom they may have defined simply as co-workers.) There are very practical implications in this train of argument. It can be supposed with considerable plausibility that the exposure of the worker to the large-scale, bureaucratised setting of the Luton plants would, for the reasons discussed in the previous chapter, account for the paradox found there. It must be said again, that in the light of their unusually heterogeneous social and geographical origins, their want of roots in the locality, and their uncommonly favourable market situation, the Luton sample turned on an impressive display of 'traditional' class consciousness. Money looms large in this consciousness — but then, it does for most people, and this is not in itself evidence for an economistic *mode* of consciousness. Provided unrealistic standards of comparison are not invoked, the affluent workers can be fairly said to reveal both solidarism and 'power', or 'us-them', imagery in a quite unambiguous way. If the Labour Party is not seen as 'the party of the class to which I belong', at least it is perceived as 'the party for working-class people like me'. Three-quarters of the men agreed, moreover, that 'there is one law for the rich and another for the poor'; and two-thirds of them considered that big business had too much power (Goldthorpe *et al.* 1968a;26-7).

The answer to the paradox, then, would be that the work situation at Luton was in fact highly conducive to class-conscious attitudes. Particularly interesting in this connection is the fact that Lockwood, in his earlier writings (including the theoretical groundwork for the affluent-worker volumes) emphasised in extremely forceful terms the primacy of the work situation in structuring social attitudes. And certainly, the contrast between sociability and solidarity just mentioned raises legitimate and serious doubts about the influence of neighbourhood relationships on images of *society*. Putting it another way, Lockwood insists (1966:252) that the 'them' of the proletarian consciousness includes 'the public authorities of the wider society'. Now it is hard to see how this would enter into the social consciousness of a closed, inward looking community except through work. Furthermore, the 'us-them' imagery is not a given of any work situation as such, or indeed of any social setting. Moore (1975) shows that in the Durham mining villages he studied 'us' may often have been taken to include miners *and* owners. The owners were local men in a relatively small way of business, and their relationships with the workforce were of the paternalistic kind, powerfully reinforced by Methodism which united both owners and the union leaders in a non-conflictual, organismic view of society and industrial relations. Thus miners often developed notions of market interests related to the fate of their *industry, not their class*, because the (frequently sharp) clashes between miners and owners were experienced within a normative frame of reference inimical to class identification. Because the 'them' of the proletarian consciousness is identified by Lockwood in specific class terms as 'bosses, managers, white-collar workers, and, ultimately, the public authorities of the larger society', the 'us-them' imagery is not so innocent of ideology as Lockwood claims. Although he wished to keep the question of political allegiances and beliefs analytically separate from that of social imagery, we really are led to infer that the proletarian traditionalist would provide a ready recruit for leftist parties. In fact, Labour made very little headway among the miners in these villages until after World War I. The tensions between the historical and sociological categories in the Luton study are therefore no accident.

Two crucial conclusions flow from this, which affect not only an understanding of Lockwood's typology but also our whole way of looking at changes in capitalist class structures. In the first place, the growth in the scale of enterprise has been an outstanding feature of capitalist industrial organisation. Between 1935 and 1963, in the British private manufacturing sector, the proportion of the labour force employed in enterprises of more than 5,000 rose from 21.1 to 42.8 percent. If it is correct to suggest that the work situation is the strongest experiential influence on class attitudes, then there has been a strong pressure from this source against any diminution of class identity — to put it no stronger. For the new industrial structure has not just broken up the habitat of the proletarian traditionalist, itself an event of ambivalent consequences for class consciousness, but it has also, and on a far greater scale, destroyed the work environment which nurtured the deferential traditionalist. Secondly, it is plain that much more specific analysis is required of the way in which class ideologies are transmitted and become integrated as part of the individual's world-view. The relation between 'situation' and 'ideology' may be changed from *either* side of the equation. More than this, says Lockwood, he has never claimed (1975:250). Seen in this light, the privatised worker presents possibilities not explored at all in the Luton study. His social consciousness is quite compatible with appeals to solidarity and radicalism, or indeed with any sort of ideology whatsoever. Unlike the other two ideal types, his day-to-day life offers no clues to the formation of distinct imagery at all: his mind is at home. But another obvious likelihood is that unionism supplies the elements of a class ideology, since unions occupy a strategic position between the individual at work and wider political processes. Hamilton (1967:278) found that unions 'constitute the most important influence on working-class politics' in his study of France. And since the C.G.T. (the Communist controlled union) dominates the big, expanding affluent plants, the French workers have become radicalised, not privatised. In England too, Coates and Silburn report (1973:166), it is the affluent, unionised segments of the working class who have the highest aspirations for themselves and their children. Goldthorpe and his team themselves contrast the optimistic, forward-looking temper of the new working class with the fatalism of traditional workers. Evidently, then, demands for more money do have a *meaning*. The insistence on 'economism' as a mode of consciousness is anyway suspect, since all wage bargaining has a context. The claims of occupational groups like the miners in Britain in recent years for enormous pay rises have been unmistakeably political challenges, set as they were in the climate of legislative restraint and appeals to the Dunkirk spirit (see Westergaard and Resler 1975:418). Finally, its worth recording that to locate the proletarian traditionalist in the stable, inbred, gregarious community Lockwood sketches for us runs counter to a tradition which has traced the bedrock of class consciousness to periods of general social upheaval. One could argue that it was just as that form of community fell apart that the possibilities of a radical meaning-system taking hold became real. Certainly, miners, shipbuilders, and steelworkers all had in common that they suffered disastrously from Britain's loss of world domination of the capitalist markets, a domination which had been founded largely on their industries and skills.

Parkin is sceptical of treating the affluent worker as in any way a special case. His concept of the subordinate meaning-system accepts the contradictions found in the affluent-worker responses as typical manifestations of a contradiction in working-class experience. Workers think that big business has too much power; but they say the same about trade unions. However, Parkin points out, in the second case, it more often than not indicates no real hostility to trade unions. Rather, it is a superficial deference to the conventional wisdom of the 'public', dominant meaning-system. This is only a way of saying that the subordinate meaning-system is ambiguous in its implications for class action because the latent possibilities for class consciousness remained unfocussed. A very important feature of this normative ambivalence, therefore, is that working-class organisations could fuse disparate, half-articulated discontents and aspirations, and so impose structure and purpose on working-class politics.

Michels on Parties

In his essay (1967) on working-class Tories, Parkin has argued that to ask why about one-third of the working-class electors are 'deviant', Conservative voters is the wrong question. Given the pervasiveness of elite values, and the relative paucity of resources (both material and symbolic) available to the opposition parties, it makes at least as much sense to enquire as to why the working class contributes so heavily to Labour support. The appeal of alternative meaning-systems, he concludes, is conditional upon the process of the 'insulation' of working-class enclaves, along the lines indicated by Lockwood. But the meaning-system itself cannot be taken for granted. That is why, in Parkin's analysis of the formation of the subordinate meaning-system, the main weight of argument falls decisively on those autonomous developments in left-wing parties which have robbed the labour movement of ideology and leadership.

Following Michels, Parkin (1972:128-36) identifies a crucial early stage in the life of left-wing parties when their growing size and influence leads to the embourgeoisement of the proletarian leadership and to bureaucratisation. This in turn makes the party more attractive to moderate leaders of middle-class origin, who use the party apparatus to further their own interests and careers, while at the same time supplying the organisation, ideology and symbols of legitimacy necessary to an alternative government. By a cumulative process of accommodation the party comes to embrace 'meritocratic' rather than 'egalitarian' socialism. That is, the emphasis shifts away from aims of equality of condition towards those urging some measure of equality of opportunity. At this point, the working-class party becomes quite acceptable to the dominant class, since the existence of competition within the framework of acceptance of the general distribution of resources poses no threat to the basic principles of capitalist order. Michels (as did Weber) took the view that *radical* working-class movements owed their origins in large part to middle-class intellectuals — Marx would be an outstanding example of the type. He was very suspicious of the idea that, left to themselves, working-class organisations could ever achieve more than an undirected, reactive opposition based on immediate grievances. In fact, Michels held such a poor opinion of the potentialities of the working class for visionary and determined leadership that he considered the proletarianisation of the elite of the labour movement as a sign of weakness, not of strength. It is necessary here, Parkin points out (1972:131), to draw a distinction between the initial de-radicalisation of working-class parties, and their subsequent development. The founders of socialism arrayed themselves on the side of the working class from a deep intellectual and moral conviction not demanded of middle-class recruits when the labour movement became respectable and offered a career rather than a cause. The critical phase in this transformation, according to Michels, came just when the radical party achieved power and recognition within the state. The case of the German party evidently impressed him particularly. Whereas the persecuted, embryo party in 1871 had had the courage and temerity to denounce what it saw as Bismarckian imperialism and war-mongering, in 1914 the leaders almost fell over themselves in an effort to prove themselves more patriotic, more nationalistic than their political enemies, thus entirely deserting the principles of proletarian internationalism for which it had always stood. The party had become a giant, but a docile one. (The metaphor is deliberately chosen, because the 'head' and 'body' analogy runs right through Michels' work.)

Although the fate of the socialist parties diverged sharply after 1918, Michels' analysis is still interesting for the period before 1914, and has much relevance for the understanding of those countries where the labour movement developed in conditions of relative political freedom, for this freedom, of course, is the precondition of the growth of the party into a mass, bureaucratised political machine. As Schumpeter emphasises (1947:320 ff.), Marx had provided little clue as to the strategies appropriate to the parties claiming his as their inspiration, beyond recommending a policy of non-cooperation except in special circumstances where scientific analysis showed that acquiescence would hasten capitalism's down-fall. It was scarcely a sufficient prescription for the complex circumstances in which the European socialist parties found themselves around the turn of the century. Any sane judgment had to concede that the evolution of capitalism showed no signs of driving the proletariat into a revolutionary posture. Three broad kinds of solution are open to a revolutionary party in such circumstances. The first is to advocate and work for the violent overthrow of the state, and so to invite immediate and condign repression. The second is to close ranks, while awaiting the moment to emerge as the leader of mass discontent, which requires the sort of patience not common in political activists, as well as great faith in one's methods of scientific analysis. The third is to try actively to win support by campaigning democratically on issues related to working-class interests, and run the risk of being a force for compromise with capitalism. Lenin chose a combination of the first two courses; but then, all marxists were agreed that Russia was a special case, and anyway the choice was not really Lenin's, but the consequence of the autocracy which ruled the Russian state. In any case, the Leninist line, which produced the fateful split between the Mensheviks and Bolsheviks, smacks of orthodoxy only in retrospect. It was unlikely to appeal to the German party, the pride of the international left, whose leaders took it for granted that strength lay with its own massed working class on which the hopes of a European revolution were largely pinned. The process of ideological revisionism initiated by Bernstein was not by any means conservative in intention. On the contrary, it represented an attempt to bridge the gap between the party leadership and its mass base. As Schumpeter's dry aside has it (1947:347), 'Trade-union leaders shrugged their shoulders and murmured about the chewing of the doctrinal cud. They had been revisionists all along.'

Once embarked upon, however, the process of accommodation becomes harder and harder to arrest. To seek mass support demands an immediate programme as well as long-term aims, and requires therefore a willingness to operate within the existing political framework. The universal franchise can be seen as a decisive event in the life of these parties, because it made such a policy feasible — and after all Marx himself was never quite able to make up his mind about the significance of the vote in the development of class relations. Given even a modicum of success in fighting for practical causes, revisionism becomes increasingly legitimated through practice. Thus it is easy to envisage the party developing in the direction of a self-sustaining bureaucracy, increasingly ill-adapted to revolutionary agitation or even non-routine activity, finally reducing the leftists to a rump or excluding them from the party altogether. Once the machinery of negotiation, arbitration, fact-finding and administration becomes institutionalised (and here, for once, the phrase seems definitely useful), the party finds itself embroiled in what Lytton Strachey once called the 'fatal exactitudes of a narrow routine'. In turn, as Parkin suggests, the party's leadership increasingly attracts professional politicians, intellectuals and career bureaucrats who, in terms of occupation and social origins, have little in common with the working class. Their loyalty to that class is not necessarily either weak or hypocritical, but neither their interests nor their background is likely to predispose them to gamble with the resources of their organisation in a tight political corner. Political opposition in these circumstances becomes very much the art of the possible, of winning small tactical gains while avoiding major battles entailed by 'utopian' principles, even if those principles are officially blessed in the party's own ideology.

The demise of a more heroic, swashbuckling style of leadership is the problem which engaged Michels' attention, and he linked this transition with the size and heterogeneity of the oppositional forces. He signals this change with a fundamental terminological distinction, contrasting the tightly-knit, democratic 'party' with what he calls a 'mere organisation' (Michels 1959:376). 'Who says organisation, says oligarchy' (Michels 1959:401), and the fact of oligarchy for Michels spells conservatism. He raises the possibility that internal oligarchy may co-exist with a radical policy in relation to other institutions, only to dismiss it. At this point, Michels' argument is pychologistic rather than sociological — it shares the basic assumptions of Pareto's elite theory. The dilution of the moral force of the party is held to occur at all levels, not only among its leaders. Once the labour movement has won a foothold within the power structure, it increasingly attracts members who join for purely selfish, individualistic purposes. At the same time, the growing wealth and size of the bureaucratic machine provides a career ladder for the most able elements within the working class, who thus find an outlet for their ambitions. The need of the masses for direction and slogans finds its counterpart in the self-seeking propensities of the leadership to manipulate the constituents they formally represent. 'What was initiated by the need for organisation, administration and strategy is completed by psychological determinism' (Michels 1959:205). The individual mobility of the working-class elite weakens the radicalism of the labour movement as a whole. However, according to Michels, it does so not simply by siphoning off potential leaders from the underclass, in the manner suggested by Pareto. His argument is a stronger and more precise one, because it suggests that the working-class elite *itself* becomes an active brake upon radicalism. Unless great care is taken, Dowse and Hughes rightly stress (1972:352), the 'iron law of oligarchy' can be rendered tautological and trivial. In any organisation representing a mass membership, oligarchies must rule, because that is their function. The crucial issues are whether they rule in their *own* interests, contrary to those of the rank-and-file; whether elected leaders are, as Michels asserted, often irremoveable; and so on.

Despite the influence it has had on subsequent empirical studies, Michels' work in *Political Parties* has never really been subjected to a thoroughgoing evaluation and critique. Nor has it found any imitators: as Goldthorpe *et al.* (1969: 189) point out, the sociology of left-wing leadership is much as Michels left it. Partly this has to do with the conceptual and practical problems involved in the study of power, but it also reflects certain basic problems inherent in developing the insights of a work which is itself far from systematic and conceptually precise. Linz (1968:268) instances Michels' use of the term 'oligarchy', and suggests that it is possible to detect no less than ten characteristics which may be found in very variegated combinations and degrees within different types of formal organisation. Michels' argument darts about in a highly allusive fashion, very difficult to re-order into a manageable set of testable hypotheses. In his hands, this approach is a virtue rather than a defect, but it does on the other hand mean that *Political Parties* raises a number of very considerable problems for the analysis of 'party' in relation to labour movements, a fact which can be masked by Michels' talent for the dramatic phrase and persuasive historical illustration.

The chief of these problems is the way in which the embourgeoisement of the working-class leaders affects class consciousness and class action. Michels himself was acutely alert to the power of the state, regarding it as axiomatic that 'the forces of party, however well developed, are altogether inferior and subordinate to the forces of the government' (Michels 1959:394). The result, he argues, is that the party abandons its revolutionary ideology and loses its revolutionary will, and is 'therefore incapable of resisting the arbitrary exercise of power by the state when this power is inspired by a vigorous will'. At the same time, Michels was not impressed by a merely programmatic radicalism, remarking of the German socialists that they combined 'revolutionary terminology' with the role of 'constitutional opposition' (1959:374). In fact, it was this curious conflict between words and deeds which attracted Michels to the study of parties in the first place (Linz 1968:266). But what sort of deeds is a (definitionally) small, revolutionary party capable of in the face of the might of the state? The answer for Michels seems to be, quite simply, that it can oppose to the bitter end with the resources it has, and this is enough. It is important to appreciate that it misses the point 'if *Political Parties* is read only as the work of a disappointed democrat or a disillusioned regular member of the Social Democratic Party. In fact, the life of a syndicalist Michels makes more sense than that of a purely Marxist-socialist Michels' (Linz 1968:266). That is, Michels held it to be the proper purpose of a party to articulate and defend an alternative vision of society, something which is inevitably threatened when it becomes entangled in electioneering and trade-union bargaining. But his work does not (as might at first sight appear) provide a ready-made explanation of the decline of radical class conflict, because it is in fact a kind of swings-and-roundabout argument. What the party gains in numbers and wealth it loses in commitment to radical egalitarianism on the part of the leadership of the labour movement. The problem for the elitist party (which Michels favours) is its isolation from the masses; the problem for a 'mere organisation' is its corruption by them.

Michels' own insistence on the power of the state also raises a question of how we are to interpret the notion of embourgeoisement. The meaning of the term is not the issue, but rather how in the empirical analysis of leadership behaviour it is ever possible to distinguish between the psychological predispositions of leaders and the constraints placed upon them by the fact of capitalist power. This is particularly important, Parkin observes (1972:133), for an understanding of the action of social-democratic governments. They only survive as governments for so long as they are prepared to act constitutionally and 'responsibly', but to do this means accepting that crucial areas of decision-making, most notably in the economy, lie permanently outside the legitimate scope of government interference. Self-interest need, and may, have nothing to do with the case. Timidity, prudence, realism and a dozen other motives besides would explain their caution. Michels' characteristically epigrammatic judgment that 'power is conservative' ignores the very disparities in power which in other contexts he is concerned to stress. It is significant that in *Political Parties* Michels gives much more emphasis to the deliberate manipulation of the rank-and-file by leaders than elsewhere (Linz 1968:266). Evidently Michels swung between the kind of argument which (rightly) stresses the difficulties in the way of mass participation in decision-making, and that which asserts the domination of a clique against mass interests. It is interesting and important to know that the leaders of parties committed to democracy and equality are frequently forced to adopt organisational strategies which run counter to their expressed values. The need for centralisation and freedom of operation does give a great deal of autonomy to elected representatives. Nevertheless, it does make a difference that they *are* elected, and it is unhelpful of Michels to confuse the distinction between *de facto* oligarchy within a trade union in a democratic society, and the kind of power held by leaders in a totalitarian order, as he was prone to do (Linz 1968:267). Trade unions and parties, in the former case, are voluntary organisations which in the last analysis depend upon the ability of leaders to mobilise support, especially when they find themselves in conflict with the agencies of the state. Michels frames his iron law of oligarchy in such a way as to give no place to the social and political context of organisation as an influence on action. In fact, it is obviously very relevant to an understanding of leadership strategies to know that (say) the party is forced to operate as a clandestine, illegal force, since its activities are shaped by that fact irrespective of the internal form of its organisation. Conversely, in a democracy factionalism within large-scale organisations may be a counter to oligarchy, by providing contenders for office (Martin 1968). This shares with theorists such as Schumpeter, although on a different level, the idea that some degree of representative democracy may be assured through the conflicts of competing pressure groups.

A result of these ambiguities in Michels' argument is the appearance of a set of essentially empirical difficulties. One would expect to find in the generality of cases, for example, that the largest, most bureaucratically organised trade unions were also the most docile, whereas in fact they include the most militant. If Michels were right in supposing that the ideological vision of the labour movement comes from the socialist intelligentsia, then it should be the case that the political wing of the movement consistently occupies the position of theoretical vanguard. But this is far from being the case. While we can easily accept, therefore, the notion that an endemic tension between means and ends dogs any mass movement, it is important to be aware that Michels' weakness for hyperbole produces considerable problems for the analysis of class conflict in a wider historical and comparative setting.

Comparative Labour Movements

The limitations on Michels' work can best be discussed initially in the context of his own favourite example, the Social Democratic Party in Germany. Between 1906 and 1909, the party underwent a very rapid process of formal structuring under Ebert, a process which was paralleled by the growing domination of the revisionist wing within the party machine at large. Revisionism, which was based on the small-town, artisan, relatively conservative element in the S.D.P., successfully imposed its policies on the radical urban centres by means of a highly undemocratic party constitution which denied proportional representation to the massed working-class enclaves. Thus, for instance, a revisionist sat in the Reichstag for left-wing Stuttgart, despite his rank unpopularity in the city. This was possible because of the gross disparities between the representation of the Stuttgart membership and the rural communities of the *Land* in which the city was situated (Schorske 1955:130-1). While we may agree in broad terms about the kind of evolution through which the party went in these years, however, it is much less clear that we can draw the same sort of general conclusions as Michels about cause and effect relationships in mass parties generally. Quite a different lesson can be derived from the situation Schorske describes, which is that radicalism can easily be suffocated if its protagonists allow the management of mundane affairs to be sacrificed to doctrinal controversy. The revisionists did not act *unconstitutionally*, and their predominance in policy formation can be attributed more to default by the radical wing than to their own talent for machination. The fact is, Schorske argues (1955:127), that the rapid increase in the number of paid officials of the S.D.P. was much less significant than Michels believed. More to the point, Ebert's organisational changes occurred at a moment when the radical wing of the party was in disarray, so that the new officialdom entered a party already committed to capturing as large a vote as possible. The nub of Michels' argument is that no party which succumbs to oligarchy can pursue a radical policy within society at large. But one might equally well argue that an unrepresentative party structure can be appropriated by radicals rather than conservatives. Furthermore, while a party dedicated to campaigning among the masses could be expected to increase its paid staff, the essentially political decision must precede such bureaucratic growth.

The process of de-radicalisation in the German party was never at any time as clear-cut as Michels' liked to maintain. Marx's attack upon the Gotha Programme in 1875 showed how far the S.D.P. had already moved in the direction of reformism under the influence of its first-phase middle-class leaders. By that date, broadly speaking, the party had abandoned the Marxian analysis of revolution in favour of the sort of demands for universal suffrage by secret ballot which the Chartists had advanced a generation earlier in England. It was Bismarck who created the revolutionary party, by introducing in 1878 twelve years of systematic repression which left no choice but to go underground (Schorske 1955:3). It was the coercive power of the state, not the social origins of the party leaders, which kept the party uncontaminated. By making it clear that under no circumstances would the S.D.P. leaders be allowed a share in power, their policy of no cooperation was assured. Nonetheless the Erfurt Programme of 1891 was itself 'designed for a non-revolutionary period, one in which the working class was growing in numbers and political self-awareness, but was still too weak to make a serious bid for power' (Schorske 1955:6). Kautsky, the party theoretician, wrote the Programme in two parts. Part I envisaged the socialist transformation of society, but as a long-term aim, and one which entailed no statement about how this was to be achieved. Part II merely expressed the interests of the working class within the existing order. The split between the radical and revisionist wings of the German labour movement did not reflect merely a process of ossification within the party. It was more the outcome of the failure of intellectuals to offer a coherent strategy under circumstances when alternative courses of action were opened up by restitution of rights of association and organisation after 1890. Equally, the endorsement in 1914 of the government's decision to go to war was by no means the kind of tame surrender which Michels appears to imply. An initially very powerful rejection of the decision by the party executive was itself upset by the return of the three most conservative members from holiday, and it came as the climax of a mounting drive against the left which the outbreak of war only brought to a head. As Michels acknowledged (1959:393), the state in wartime arrogates particularly sweeping powers. True, the trade unions quickly made a compact with the state in return for a guarantee of their existence during wartime. But the threat of military dictatorship, fear of defeat by Russia, and the nagging possibility that they would find themselves without working-class support, all contributed to the final capitulation by the leaders (Schorske 1955:288 ff).

Michels held that no revolutionary party can realise its aims by constitutional means, by winning a majority in parliamentary bodies. Put like this, the argument is in many ways a persuasive one. It somewhat parallels Lenin's view of the role of revolutionary *cadres*, whose business it is to keep ideology and strategy honed, to take every advantage of the weakness of the party's bourgeois enemies by channelling mass discontents into action. However, there is no corresponding emphasis in Michels on *action*; ultimately, it is never really clear what the party is *for*, except to preserve the 'soul' of the labour movement, 'its doctrinal and theoretic content' (Michels 1959:374). What comes across quite unambiguously is an absolute distaste for any form of compromise, with the result that Michels' elitist proclivities make him less than just to the achievements of reformist leaders.

Bauman's study (1972) of the British labour movement makes it clear that, in this case at least, moderate, bureaucratically organised unionism was the cause, not the effect, of its mass character. Political radicalism did emerge from the first capitalist proletariat in the early nineteenth century, in the shape of Chartism. Although Chartism commanded wide support, however, it mysteriously fizzled out in a rainstorm in 1848, and this was symbolic of the entire working-class movement during the preceding period. That is, although in the early phases of industrialisation there grew up genuine class organisations, such as the Grand National Consolidated Trade Union, embracing hundreds of thousands of disaffected proletarians, their existence was wholly ephemeral. They survived for only a matter of a few months, and their persistent collapse severely damaged the morale of the working class and its will to organise (Bauman 1972:48-9). The secret of this instability, Bauman suggests, is the atomised character of the working class which organisers had to contend with

Quite simply, it lacked that grounding in 'community' which could sustain a long struggle for enlarged rights. The newly-bred, rootless proletariat was easily mobilised for sporadic mass movements (such as Luddism), but it lacked staying power. Trade unionism first took on some of its modern characteristics in the organisations of skilled artisans, built upon their sense of occupational identification. The contradictions of the growth of the labour movement are well illustrated by this fact since, as noted earlier, the craft unions in many respects split the working class. Skilled men formed a labour aristocracy, which while not necessarily petty-bourgeois in mentality, certainly looked down on the disorganised, unskilled mass of the working class. On another level, however, this type of unionism was a powerful example of what could be achieved through organisation, and injected a qualitatively new kind of leadership into the working-class elite. Bauman traces out the demise of the charismatic phase of union struggle, and the emergence of a 'second generation' of union leaders — men, roughly speaking, who were powerful within the movement around 1870, when the unions achieved legal recognition.

> 'While they in no way conformed to the model of the popular charismatic leader so often encountered in earlier decades, they were none the less strong and outstanding men in their own way, men of iron who, in an exceptionally unfavourable climate of opinion, forced through the new conception of legal and loyal trade unions which were essential if capitalist society was to function normally. They were the first men of working class origin in Britain to succeed in the difficult task of constructing trade union organisations that were not only complex and extensive but also lasting and stable' (Bauman 1972:116).

These men were not demagogues, but exceptionally gifted administrators. And they were certainly not remarkable for their dedication to the principles of internal democracy. Quite the contrary: they seem to have been in many respects 'shaped by contemporary capitalist society to conform to and resemble the positive heroes of the society — the businessmen' (Bauman 1972:117). The virtues of these new-style leaders, and their vices, curiously resembled those of their opponents. They combined energy, foresight and organising abilities of a high order with some fair degree of autocracy and ruthlessness, in many instances. Furthermore, the traits they encouraged in their followers were those of thrift, sobriety and industriousness in the service of employers. Above all, their aim was to achieve respectability and acceptance by the governing classes. From one angle, such a strategy was necessarily accommodative, if by this is meant that it did not have a revolutionary programme. It was also a pre-condition of any practical advances towards working-class political and industrial power, and the opposition it generated, although ideologically moderate, was tough and brought results.

The collapse of the specifically political Chartist agitation, and the emergence of the moderate craft unionism just described naturally meant that the piecemeal enfranchisement of the more respectable elements of the working class became a quite acceptable strategy. Even the Tories, particularly as they came under the influence of Disraeli, were willing to compete for the support of these groups, and did so with conspicuous success. But it was the liberals who provided the natural avenue of influence for the trade unions, and gave labour its first parliamentary representatives. Liberal political philosophy was not opposed to trade unions, always provided they did not threaten free trade or private property. In fact, the unions had a very obvious use as channels of communication and organisation, and employers often acknowledged this quite explicitly. This alliance was a perfectly natural one, since in the conditions of mid-Victorian society the middle strata included not only shopkeepers and artisans, but many small-scale entrepreneurs as well. The owners were local men, familiar with and concerned by the conditions of their employees. Then, as now, it was the great cities which were the focus of radicalism. Sometimes, as the work of Moore shows (1975), this perception of common interests and the interdependence of owners and labour was powerfully reinforced by a shared faith, Methodism. Although there is no reason at all to suppose that Methodism acted on the masses as a kind of surrogate socialism, it bound union *leaders* and their opponents into a common religious fellowship which precluded a conflictual view of society. Of course, how far Methodism had the major impact claimed for it by Halevy remains a highly contentious issue.

What happened in effect, then, was that the radical potential of the working class was short circuited by a reformist trade-union movement. To say this is not to subscribe to a Michelsian view of social movements, but simply to point out that once by dint of favourable circumstances the reformist wing achieved legal status and the right of campaigning for membership, a radical shift became much less probable. The most articulate and politically resourceful segments of labour were no longer available to lead it. Furthermore, with the resurgence of popular unrest towards the end of the century, a strong institutionalised labour organisation was there to spearhead the new attack. A new wave of tough, militant leaders such as Tom Mann and Keir Hardie led the previously unorganised working class, but they were themselves the product of a reformist tradition, so that their public language was not that of socialists as the theorists of the German S.D.P. understood the term. The fact that the reformist leadership became stabilised before contact was made with international socialism is itself possibly a matter of some importance. It is quite clear that the representatives sent to the meetings of the International knew little and cared less about the seething doctrinal controversies that went on there, and brought nothing in the way of ideological radicalism back with them. Whether they would have been better leaders if they had is, of course, a moot point.

The differences in character between labour movements are sufficiently marked and of such long standing as to suggest to some sociologists that we should pay a great deal more attention to the structure of the society in which industrialisation took place (see on this Moore 1969, for a very fine example of a sweeping comparative survey). Thus, both Giddens and Mann argue that the (in Gidden's phrase) 'post-feudal' period is a crucial point of transition, for here an uprooted rural peasantry experience the shock of transplantation into the industrial workforce. There is a body of empirical evidence which shows that uprootedness leads to a volatility that may feed extremist politics of the right or the left. Communist support in France, for example, draws on rural radicalism (Hamilton 1967:275). Whether or not working-class politics take on a leftward shift is partly determined by the pre-industrial political influences at work in any given society, partly by the strength of left-wing organisation at the point of destination (Mann 1973: 40-1). Whether opposition takes on a specifically *socialist* tinge will also depend on other, in part contingent, factors of the kind which propelled the German and British labour movements in different directions. What is more, the argument continues, the kind of configuration of economy and polity that emerges from this period of upheaval tends to become 'frozen' — Giddens again. This idea is used by Mann as a means of explaining the fact that in Latin Europe an ideologically radical mass party has survived to this day. The mark of 'true capitalists' is held to consist in the fact that they 'content themselves with a bureaucratic, economically-based mode of control over their workforce' (Mann 1973:41). Severe conflict is likely to arise when capitalists try to rule through what end-of-ideologists sometimes call a 'total ideology', one which brings up ethical issues difficult to compromise. As an example of what he means, Mann cites the case of French and Italian employers who cling to quasi-feudal rights in their management practices. They flirt with fascism, and have no truck with unions, and so fuel extremism:

> 'In the development of industrial relations the initiative, and most of the power, lies with the employer and the government. If they take the path of compromise and adopt the language of market bargaining, then working-class economistic and reformist tendencies are greatly strengthened. It is the growth of capitalist hegemony that has produced a decline in socialist ideology in some countries' (Mann 1973:42).

Capitalist hegemony means what Weber called capitalism's ethic of 'disenchantment', the cash nexus. The persistence of ideologically radical working-class parties is to be understood as the product of 'cultural' factors – such as religious cleavages — superimposed upon class divisions.

This line of reasoning appears fleetingly in Dahrendorf's work (1959), for whom the term 'superimposition' in relation to the various institutional spheres is the key to the intensity of social conflict. However, both Mann and Giddens rightly reject the possibility of applying a unitary model to the development of capitalist societies. This holds out the pleasant prospect of a more extensive typology of working-class movements, and one which in Mann's case involves an interesting and ambitious attempt at the *dynamic* analysis of class consciousness. Unfortunately, this enterprise gets bogged down by the fact that the notions of 'reformist' and 'revolutionary' ideologies, a reasonable enough conceptual contrast in itself, become linked to specific political cultures. That is, the institutional forms established in (say) France during its post-feudal phase create the basis of greater political radicalism, and so on. A dichotomy is obviously preferable to a unitary scheme, but it is a great pity if the advantages of flexibility won methodologically are squandered empirically. Furthermore, these two theorists do not really escape the evolutionary trap which they see as having swallowed up others. What they both want to do is to invert Marx, and to argue that 'mature' capitalism produces, not a revolution, but exactly that sort of economistic accommodation which is the essence of the institutionalisation of class conflict (Mann 1973:43; Giddens 1973:287). This has the advantage of requiring the theorist to explain the presence of class consciousness, not its absence, but it raises other rather serious difficulties.

What are we to make of the claim that the post-feudal phase of capitalist societies sees the emergence of 'basic elements' of social order, which then remain 'highly resistant' to change (Giddens 1973:214)? The industrial revolution was no doubt a change so cataclysmic as to stand permanently as a special case in sociological theory, but just the same other things have happened since then. To take the case of Germany once more, the labour movement has experienced nothing but change of a fundamental variety. In the imperial era it was alternately suppressed or outshone all the others in power and prestige. Following its submission in 1914, the S.D.P. found itself at the end of the war leading (sometimes rather unwillingly) a defeated state, and by the end of the twenties had been swamped by the mass appeal of communism. Hitler then smashed the left through brutal repression, while a decade later the victorious democracies restored a reformist organisation of labour which imitated their own. Italy's history was remarkably similar. Mann asks himself what importance we are to give to 'external' influences like these (but does not give the answer). They had a great deal of influence in many instances. The quotation marks are his own (Mann 1973:43), but they do not remove the problem of how we can label such factors as 'external' at all. The fact is, Hamilton and Wright point out (1975:32), that it is possible to expend too much energy devising theories to account for things which are very simple. Without wishing to deny all validity to the case made out by Mann and Giddens, this can be argued for radicalism in France, to which both attach considerable theoretical importance.

It is quite true that political radicalism has been endemic in France since 1789, and equally true that some contemporary features of French society fit into the line of direct descent from Jacobinism (Mann 1973:41). A simple instance of the phenomenon which Mann has in mind occurs in Italy, where communist support is still heavily concentrated in the 'red belt' of Emilia and Tuscany, just those areas which nourished the strong anarchist movement of a century ago. In France, though in a more complex fashion, an analogous pattern of rural radicalism can be mapped out, going even further back into the past. This obviously suggests that, under some circumstances, it may be *radicalism*, not reformism, that becomes 'institutionalised': this is just the point that Mann and Giddens are urging. Nevertheless, it is misleading to imply that French radicalism is, so to speak, a continuous affair, attributable to the same fundamental constellation of causes. On the contrary, it can be argued very strongly that on balance the two major clues to an understanding of the character of radicalism in twentieth-century France lie in war and the October Revolution.

The founding of the French Communist Party in 1920 was itself in crucial respects a profound break with the past. French socialism up till 1914 was dominated by the anarchist branch of the International, and from about 1900 the labour movement followed the revolutionary-syndicalist line set by the C.G.T. In many ways, the French anarchists expressed Michels' ideal in action. Small in numbers because it only accepted activists, the party was linked, not organisationally, but chiefly through its journals and the activities of its distinguished intellectuals (Woodcock 1975:277). Nevertheless, a large minority of the C.G.T. was reformist, and the organisation itself did not represent a majority of French workers; already revolutionary influences were on the wane by 1908. When war broke out, the anarchists too went to war, and the movement, having no organisational base, evaporated. The success of the Bolsheviks split the C.G.T. further, by providing an attraction for the anarchist activists with which syndicalism could not compete. Many joined the P.C.F. (Woodcock 1975:302-6). Meanwhile, the Communists succeeded, at the Congress in Lyons in 1920, in annexing most of the support of the S.F.I.O., the French Section of the International. Almost overnight, France acquired a party organised along Leninist lines, and with a massive trade-union base through which to work.

Because the P.C.F. was Moscow-controlled, its support in the inter-war years fluctuated with the labyrinthine shifts of policy imposed by Stalin's diplomacy. The details of these twists and turns are not in themselves important. The point being made here is that a large part of the analysis can be carried out in terms of the operation of unique events. Thus, to take one more important example, World War II strengthened communist influence very greatly, partly because of the honourable role played by many of its members in the Resistance, partly because when the Liberation came the party was one of the few organisations left in France capable of decisive action. De Gaulle brought Thorez back from Moscow to help in the work of reconstruction, since the traditional political rulers of France were either decimated or tainted by collaboration. In the period of relative peace and stability since then, however, the mass following of the party has dropped off consistently. There was a very rapid decline both in memership and in the circulation of the party press after the onset of the Cold War. Stalinism and Soviet imperialism in Eastern Europe were a constant drain on goodwill, especially among the middle classes. The very big and influential teachers' union broke away from the C.G.T. largely because of the Moscow connection, and it is generally true of both the P.C.F. and its satellite union that their 'rigid, intransigent, political character made affiliation unattractive and problematic for many members' (Hamilton 1967:283; see also Clark 1967:72).

Again, viewing the world too much *sub specie aeternitatis* may deflect attention from the *specific* mechanisms associated with 'reformism', and so in turn from trends which undermine the institutionalised compromise obtaining at any particular time. The single most striking fact about the development of the American labour movement until well into this century was that it was built up from waves of immigrants.

> 'During the era of the great migrations, over 25 million people settled in this country, more than half of whom arrived between 1900 and 1914. By the end of World War I, immigrants and their children composed 38.4 percent of the population.... About three-fourths of them lived in urban areas' (Parenti 1968:81).

The social consequences of this influx reflected its immense scale. American capitalism, which in its early phases had shown signs of proceeding in a highly planned and sedate fashion, produced all the outward signs of misery in its industrial cities, but without any of the same overt unrest. To a very large extent, this could be ascribed to the deep ethnic cleavages among the immigrants themselves. In addition, so many of them brought the assumptions and outlook of a backward, conservative peasantry that adherence to leftist politics was a most improbable outcome of even the severest deprivation. Last but not least, the cultural and linguistic barriers between the immigrants and the indigenous working classes who might have acted as leaders were insurmountable. First, the native-born were heavily concentrated in the skilled working class, and were themselves unionists of an essentially conservative kind. But what really settled the issue was that the immigrants constituted — or at the least were seen as constituting — an economic threat. More than any other country at that time, the United States was characterised by a 'split' labour market (see Bonacich 1972), which both fed and was nourished by ethnic divisions and prejudices. By means of devices such as exorbitantly high entrance fees and examinations in which those whose language was not English could not hope to pass, the unions built up an exclusionist policy based on control of the supply of labour to the better paid trades (Mackenzie 1973:173).

At the same time as the British working class was experiencing a two-step phase of integration under a vigorous trade-union leadership, the ranks of American labour experienced quite the opposite: a fragmentation quite unparalleled in any contemporary capitalist state. The result, suggests Parenti, was Tammany Hall, the urban political machine which flourished especially between 1875 and 1940. Of course, no single factor will ever account for something as complex as this very American institution, but it certainly cannot be denied that the presence of large, socially and politically isolated ethnic communities lent it a great deal of its rationale. What developed from this was 'a crude, inefficient, and frequently corrupt improvisation of a social welfare system, involving a minor redistribution of income' (Parenti:1968:90). That is to say, to people who would otherwise have had nowhere to turn, the ward-captain could offer a helping hand in return for political support. The local club performed the function pre-empted elsewhere by Friendly Societies and trade unions — and it distributed no message of working-class solidarity and dissent with its practical favours. It is interesting to note, incidentally, that Michels reserved his most vituperative passage for his descriptions of the American labour leaders, claiming (1959:312) that in very many cases their loyalties had been bought. This may well be true of the period about which we are speaking, but it has nothing to do with the evils of compromise as such. In a way, the American working class got just the leadership it deserved, for nowhere was there any institutionalised support for enlightened reform, let alone socialist programmes. The Democrats, although now the beneficiaries of a high proportion of working-class and minority-group votes, has never been a labour party in the European sense of that term. Weber, writing in the early years of the century, was one of those who commented on the total lack of ideological conflict between the two vote-catching machines.

A generation later Roosevelt asked for support for the New Deal as a way of averting revolution. Rhetoric aside, the depression was cause enough for genuine alarm. The second-generation immigrant workers were no longer beyond the reach of union organisers, and the central feature of the period was the meteoric rise of the Confederation of Industrial Organisations, which seceded from the craft-dominated American Federation of Labour in 1935. The C.I.O. used militant tactics and proved extraordinarily successful. Detroit, which until the late thirties was a non-union city, became one overnight: 'workers literally swarmed into the union halls' (Leggett 1968:49). There is very little doubt that the C.I.O. in fact could have provided the organisational base for linking the Socialist Party to a mass base, since its leaders included political action among their aims and were themselves in many cases affiliated to the party. The Socialists, under Norman Thomas, bungled this opportunity with an idiotic compromise which, like everything they did during his reign, failed either to bring practical gain or reinforce ideological principle:

> 'When the young trade-unionists, whom the socialists seeded into the labor movement, faced the necessity of going along politically with Roosevelt and the New Deal in order to safeguard progressive legislative gains, the socialists

> proposed a "labor party", rather than work with the Democrats, and so the Socialist Party lost almost its entire trade-union base' (Bell 1960:288).

The employers played into the hands of working-class militant organisations with some of the nastiest tactics even in a labour history notorious for violent confrontations. They used every means of repression available, from finks (agents provocateurs) to private police forces. The La Follette committee set up to investigate these troubles turned up the information that the employers controlled more arms than the Chicago police (Dahrendorf 1959:135). Nonetheless, the trade unions won major concessions concerning their right to consultation over labour problems and their right to organise. Furthermore, the 1928 presidential election signalled the alignment of urban, working-class America with the Democratic Party, a split cemented in 1936 when the world of business entered into a much more definitive alliance with the Republicans. Class-based politics had come to America.

As to the rightness of the overall theoretical shift in emphasis proposed by Giddens and Mann, there can be little quarrel. It is quite pointless to persist in the assumption that the lack of radicalism in working-class politics generally is something requiring special explanation, precisely because it is a general phenomenon. There is a definite attraction in the claim that the result of political incorporation of the working classes 'has not been to weaken, but to stabilise, or complete, the institutional mediation of power in the capitalist order' (Giddens 1973:285). While the struggles of wage labour were linked with issues concerning civic freedom and political equality, class conflict was necessarily politicised. Not only were these relatively simple issues on which to build a mass movement, they also drew (especially in England and France) on the liberal traditions of bourgeois society. The granting of rights of citizenship and of collective bargaining, however, effectively snaps the link, save where it is preserved by socialist parties as part of a critique of private property. Under reformist leaders, therefore, industrial conflict characteristically narrows to 'aggressive economism and defensive control'

(Mann 1973:21). In a word, conflict is institutionalised. Political and industrial struggles are pursued in isolation from one another, and even matters relating to job control on the shop floor (which involve sensitive questions of managerial prerogatives) are abandoned in return for monetary gains. Arguing in the same vein, Parkin (1972:91) asserts that collective bargaining by trade unions legitimates the reward-structure, and that the legal protection afforded trade unions, and the social honours bestowed on their leaders, are evidence that the teeth of the labour movement have been drawn.

This is true as far as it goes, but it does not go quite far enough. Above all, it is essential to insist that the possibility of reformism taking serious and systematic root in the working class is continually threatened by the underlying anarchy (in its strict meaning) of the capitalist market. The institutions and mentality appropriate to routinised class relationships depend on the kind of stability which capitalism is peculiarly unfitted to providing. It is not just a question of the wars and slumps, although (as the discussion of the American labour movement shows) they may, within a remarkably short space of time, have a powerful radicalising effect. The point is rather that the *normal* operation of capitalist societies tends to reproduce in a continuous cycle the kind of problems which effectively prevent a wholesale de-politicisation. That is, trade-unionism is still concerned, and necessarily so, with human and social problems which go well beyond a routinised economism, however much the ideological pronouncements of the union movement lack in incisiveness. As Coates and Silburn have put it (1973:218-9), in a simple but effective way, any trade-union movement based on self-interest would melt away as a result of the power within it of the more skilled, relatively affluent workers. The fact is that unions spend much less time in dividing the spoils among their members than trying to reconcile or avoid splits between contending groups, attempting to ward off redundancies, to improve the position of low-paid workers, and so on. It is not narrowness or sloth which is the fundamental problem, but the fact that the rules of collective bargaining are not of the Queensberry type, and require a sustained effort by the union movement to maintain. Parkin might have added that, as well as giving knighthoods, governments (including Labour ones) set up industrial courts and pass hostile legislation above and beyond the sort of legal obstructionism normally experienced by labour leaders. Clearly, then, the institutionalisation of class conflict is always a somewhat precarious matter

In fact, union concern with bread-and-butter problems can be seen as a highly rational ordering of priorities, both from the standpoint of the members' interests and from that of the leadership, which must try to preserve the organisational base of class action under far from easy conditions. Certainly, the trade union movement is dominated by leaders whose first priority is securing economic benefits for their members, and in order to do this they must cooperate with the institutions of capitalism. The significance of this fact cannot, however, be gauged from a comparison with a Michelsian profile of the revolutionary leader. Bureaucratised unionism is a necessary feature of the capitalist social order, but it still makes sense to ask whose ends the organisation serves. Bauman argues (1972:305) that the question of differentiation within the organisation of unions is subordinate to the web of interdependence which derived from the fact that neither leaders nor rank-and-file can move too far without the other. This structured identity of interests, he concludes, is more efficient than participatory democracy in controlling the activities of the leadership. Whatever the attachment of the elite of the labour movement to revolutionary aims, without due attention to economistic aims its power base would collapse. It is notable in this connection (at least in Britain) that the trade-union leaders are still not middle class in the sense that this is true of the higher echelons of the Labour Party. Although they spend far less time in manual work nowadays than they did 50 years ago, they continue to rise through the ranks of the hierarchy itself, and are not recruited from outside. As Weber emphasised, in many respects bureaucratisation is a virtue in political affairs. It makes for stability and efficiency, and underpins what degree of countervailing power the working class exercises on a continuous basis. The cost of this organisational base (in more senses than one sometimes) is a massive involvement in the mundane preoccupations of the workforce.

Nonetheless, one must in the last analysis agree with Mann that the labour movements seem to have lost their way. Even where, as in France, a species of radical ideology has survived and radical action has gone on, it has been in spite of a compromised and compromising leadership. In Britain, even Westergaard and Resler (1975:418), sturdy champions though they are of the latent powers of the labour movement, cannot discern anything more than a 'patchy foundation of a quasi-socialist counter-ideology' within it. Now, as always, the problem is one of finding ways of translating into a socialist strategy the sort of preoccupations and problems which arise out of working-class existence. For whether this strategy comes from intellectuals, the trade-union movement, or wherever, there can be no doubt that socialism is learned (Mann 1973:71). And the problems of carrying the lesson to push forward a mass-based, libertarian socialism are formidable indeed, while the possibilities if this is not done are ugly.

Bibliography

Abrams, P. 1972. 'The Sense of the Past and the Origins of Sociology', *Past and Present* 55.

Abrams, M. and Rose, R. 1960. *Must Labour Lose?*, London.

Allcorn, D.H. and Marsh, C.M. 1975. 'Occupational Communities — Communities of What?', in Bulmer (ed.), 1975.

Allen, V.L. 1966. *Militant Trade Unionism,* London.

Anderson, P. and Blackburn, R. (eds.) 1965. *Towards Socialism*, London.

Aron, R. 1950. 'Social Structure and the Ruling Class', *British Journal of Sociology* 1.

Aron, R. 1968. *Main Currents in Sociological Thought*, (in 2 vols.), London.

Atkinson, A.B. (ed.) 1973. *Wealth, Income and Inequality*, London.

Avineri, S. 1968. *The Social and Political Thought of Karl Marx*, Cambridge.

Bauman, Z. 1972. *Between Class and Elite*, Manchester.

Bell, D. 1960. *The End of Ideology*, New York.

Bendix, R. 1963. *Work and Authority in Industry,* New York.

Bendix, R. 1966. *Max Weber: an Intellectual Portrait*, London.

Bendix, R. and Lipset, S.M. (eds.) 1966. *Class, Status and Power*, (2nd edition), New York.

Beynon, H. and Blackburn, R.M. 1972. *Perceptions of Work*, Cambridge.

Blackburn, R. 1965. 'The New Capitalism', in Anderson and Blackburn (eds.), 1965.

Blackburn, R. and Cockburn, C. (eds.) 1967. *The Incompatibles: Trade Union Militancy and the Consensus*, London.
Blau, P.M. and Duncan, O.D. 1967. *The American Occupational Structure*, New York.
Blauner, R. 1964. *Alienation and Freedom,* Chicago.
Blauner, R. 1966. 'Work Satisfaction and Industrial Trends in Modern Society', in Bendix and Lipset (eds.), 1966.
Blondel, J. 1967. *Voters, Parties and Leaders*, (revised edition), London.
Bonacich, E. 1972. 'A Theory of Ethnic Antagonism: the Split Labor Market', *American Sociological Review* 37.
Bottomore, T. 1954. 'Social Stratification in Voluntary Organisations', in Glass (ed.), 1954.
Bottomore, T. (ed.) 1963. *Karl Marx: Early Writings*, New York.
Bottomore, T. (ed.) 1973 *Karl Marx*, Englewood Cliffs.
Bottomore, T. and Rubel, M. (eds.) 1963. *Karl Marx: Selected Writings in Sociology and Social Philosophy*, London.
Buckley, W. 1958. 'Social Stratification and the Functional Theory of Social Differentiation', *American Sociological Review* 23.
Bulmer, M. (ed.) 1975. *Working-Class Images of Society,* London.

Centers, R. 1961. *The Psychology of Social Classes*, New York.
Clark, J.M. 1967. *Teachers and Politics in France*, New York.
Coates, K. and Silburn, R. 1973. *Poverty: the Forgotten Englishmen*, London.
Cole, G.D.H. 1950. 'The Conception of the Middle Classes', *British Journal of Sociology* 1.
Cousins, J.M. and Davis, R.L. 1974. 'Working-Class Incorporation: a Historical Approach', in Parkin (ed.), 1974.
Cousins, J.M. and Davis, R.L. 1975. 'The "New Working Class" and the Old', in Bulmer (ed.), 1975.
Crozier, M. 1971. *The World of the Office Worker*, Chicago.

Dahrendorf, R. 1959. *Class and Class Conflict in an Industrial Society,* London.
Davis, K. 1948. *Human Society,* New York.
Davis, K. and Moore, W.E. 1945. 'Some Principles of Stratification', *American Sociological Review* 10.
Deverson, J. and Lindsay, K. 1975. *Voices from the Middle Class,* London.
Dowse, R.E. and Hughes, J.A. 1972. *Political Sociology*, London.

Eldridge, J.E.T. 1971. *Sociology and Industrial Life*, London.
Engels, F. 1968. *The Condition of the Working Class in England in 1844*, London.

Ford, J. 1969. *Social Class and the Comprehensive School*, London.

Gerth, H.H. and Mills, C.W. 1948. *From Max Weber*, London.
Giddens, A. 1968. '"Power" in the Recent Writings of Talcott Parsons', *Sociology* 2.
Giddens, A. 1971. *Capitalism and Modern Social Theory*, Cambridge.
Giddens, A. 1973. *The Class Structure of the Advanced Societies*, London.
Giddens, A. 1974. 'Elites in the British Class Structure', in Stanworth and Giddens (eds.), 1974.
Glass, D.V. (ed.) 1954. *Social Mobility in Britain*, London.
Goldthorpe, J.H. 1966. 'Attitudes and Behaviour of Car Assembly Workers', *British Journal of Sociology* 17.
Goldthorpe, J.H. and Lockwood, D. 1963. 'Affluence and the British Class Structure', *Sociological Review* 11.
Goldthorpe, J.H., Lockwood, D., Bechhofer, F. and Platt, J.
1968. *The Affluent Worker: Industrial Attitudes and Behaviour*, Cambridge.
1968a. *The Affluent Worker: Political Attitudes and Behaviour*, Cambridge.
1969. *The Affluent Worker in the Class Structure*, Cambridge.
Gray, R.Q. 1974. 'The Labour Aristocracy in the Victorian Class Structure', in Parkin (ed.), 1974.

Halmos, P. (ed.) 1964. *The Development of Industrial Societies: The Sociological Review Monograph No. 8*, University of Keele.
Halsey, A.H. (ed.) 1972. *Trends in British Society since 1900*, London.
Hamilton, R. 1967. *Affluence and the French Worker in the Fourth Republic*, Princeton.
Hamilton, R. 1972. *Class and Politics in the United States*, New York.
Hamilton, R. and Wright, J. 1975. *New Directions in Political Sociology*, Indianapolis.
Heller, C.S. (ed.) 1969. *Structured Social Inequality*, New York.
Hobsbawm, E.J. 1964. *Labouring Men*, London.
Hodge, R.W., Siegel, P.M. and Rossi, P.H. 1966. 'Occupational

Prestige in the United States 1925-63', in Bendix and Lipset (eds.), 1966.
Hoggart, R. 1958. *The Uses of Literacy*, London.
Huaco, G.C. 1966. 'The Functionalist Theory of Stratification: Two Decades of Controversy', *Inquiry* 9.
Hughes, J. 1968. 'The Increase in Inequality', *New Statesman*, 8 November 1968.

Ingham, G.K. 1969. 'Plant Size: Political Attitudes and Behaviour', *Sociological Review* 17.
Ingham, G.K. 1970. *Size of Industrial Organisation and Worker Behaviour*, Cambridge.

Jackson, B. and Marsden, D. 1966. *Education and the Working Class*, London.
Johnson, T.J. 1972. *The Professions and Power*, London.

Kelsall, R.K. 1954. 'Self-Recruitment in Four Professions', in Glass (ed.), 1954.
Kelsall, R.K., Poole, A., and Kuhn, A. 1972. *Graduates: the Sociology of an Elite*, London.
Kerr, C. and Siegel, A. 1954. 'The Inter-Industry Propensity to Strike', in A. Kornhauser *et al.* (eds.), *Industrial Conflict*, New York, 1954.
Kohn, M.L. 1963. 'Social Class and Parent-Child Relationships: An Interpretation', *American Journal of Sociology* 68.
Kohn, M.L. 1969. *Class and Conformity*, Dorsey.
Kolko, G. 1962. *Wealth and Power in America*, New York.

Legget, J.C. 1968. *Class, Race and Labor*, Oxford.
Linz, J. 1968. 'Michels', in *International Encyclopedia of the Social Sciences*, London.
Lipset, S.M. 1963. *Political Man*, London.
Lipset, S.M. 1969. *Revolution and Counterrevolution*, London.
Lipset, S.M. and Bendix, R. 1959. *Social Mobility in Industrial Society*, London.
Little, A.N. and Westergaard, J.H. 1964. 'The Trend of Class Differentials in Educational Opportunity in England and Wales', *British Journal of Sociology* 15.
Littlejohn, J. 1972. *Social Stratification*, London.
Lockwood, D. 1958. *The Blackcoated Worker*, London.
Lockwood, D. 1966. 'Sources of Variation in Working-Class Images

of Society', *Sociological Review* 14.
Lockwood, D. 1975. 'In Search of the Proletarian Worker', in Bulmer (ed.), 1975.
Lukes, S. 1975. *Power: a Radical View,* London.
Lupton, T. 1963. *On the Shop Floor*, Oxford.
Lupton, T. and Wilson, S. 1973. 'The Social Background of "Top Decision Makers"', in Urry and Wakeford (eds.), 1973.

Mackenzie, G. 1973. *The Aristocracy of Labor*, Cambridge.
Mackenzie, G. 1974. 'The "Affluent Worker" Study: An Evaluation and Critique', in Parkin (ed.), 1974.
McLellan, D. 1971. *The Thought of Karl Marx,* London.
McLellan, D. 1973. *Marx's Grundrisse*, St. Albans.
Mann, M. 1970. 'The Social Cohesion of Liberal Democracy', *American Sociological Review* 35.
Mann, M. 1973. *Consciousness and Action among the Western Working Class*, London.
Mannheim, K. 1960. *Ideology and Utopia*, London.
Marceau, J. 1974. 'Education and Social Mobility in France', in Parkin (ed.), 1974.
Martin, D. and Crouch, C. 1971. 'England', in M. Scotford Archer and S. Giner (eds.), *Contemporary Europe: Class, Status and Power*, London, 1971.
Martin, F.M. 1954. 'An Inquiry into Parents' Preferences in Secondary Education', in Glass (ed.), 1954.
Marx, K. 1930. *Capital*. London.
Marx and Engels: Selected Works, 1968, (in 1 vol.), London.
Marx and Engels: Collected Works, 1976, London.
MESW & MECW: see above, under *Marx and Engels, Selected (Collected) Works.*
Michels, R. 1959. *Political Parties*, New York.
Miliband, R. 1969. *The State in Capitalist Society*, London.
Miller, S.M. 1969. 'Comparative Social Mobility', in Heller (ed.), 1969.
Mills, C.W. 1956. *The Power Elite*, Oxford.
Mills. C.W. 1957. *White Collar*, Oxford.
Moore, R.S. 1975. 'Religion as a Source of Variation in Working-Class Images of Society', in Bulmer (ed.), 1975.

Pahl, J.M. and Pahl, R.E. 1971. *Managers and their Wives*, London.
Pahl, R.E. and Winkler, J.T. 1974. 'The Economic Elite: Theory and Practice', in Stanworth and Giddens (eds.), 1974.

Parenti, M. 1968. 'Immigration and Political Life', in F. C. Jaher (ed.), *The Age of Industrialism in America*, New York, 1968.

Parkin, F. 1967. 'Working-Class Conservatives: A Theory of Political Deviance', *British Journal of Sociology* 18.

Parkin, F. 1968. *Middle Class Radicalism*, Manchester.

Parkin, F. 1972. *Class Inequality and Political Order*, London.

Parkin, F. (ed.) 1974. *The Social Analysis of Class Structure*, London.

Parsons, T. 1964. *Essays in Sociological Theory,* Glencoe.

Parsons, T. 1966. 'On the Concept of Political Power', in Bendix and Lipset (eds.), 1966.

Parsons, T. 1968. 'The Professions', in *International Encyclopedia of the Social Sciences,* London.

Pen, J. 1971. *Income Distribution*, London.

Piven, F.F. and Cloward. 1972. *Regulating the Poor: the Functions of Public Welfare,* London.

Plowman, D.E.G., Minchington, W.E. and Stacey, M. 1962. 'Local Social Status in England and Wales', *Sociological Review* 10.

Raynor, J. 1969. *The Middle Class*, London.

Rex, J. 1961. *Key Problems of Sociological Theory*, London.

Rex, J. 1968. 'The Sociology of a Zone in Transition', in R.E. Pahl (ed.), *Readings in Urban Sociology*, 1968, Oxford.

Rex, J. 1974. 'Capitalism, Elites and the Ruling Class', in Stanworth and Giddens (eds.), 1974.

Robinson, J. 1949. *An Essay on Marxian Economics*, London.

Routh, G. 1965. *Occupation and Pay in Great Britain, 1906-60*, Cambridge.

Schorske, C.E. 1955. *German Social Democracy, 1905-1917*, New York.

Schumpeter, J. 1950. *Capitalism, Socialism and Democracy,* London.

Sewell, W.H., Haller, A.O. and Straus, M.A. 1957. 'Social Status and Educational and Occupational Aspiration', *American Sociological Review* 22.

Shostak, A.B. 1969. *Blue-Collar Life*, New York.

Stacey, M. 1960. *Tradition and Change: A Study of Banbury*, Oxford.

Stanworth, P. and Giddens, A. (eds.) 1974. *Elites and Power in British Society*, Cambridge.

Sykes, A.J.M. 1965. 'Some Differences in the Attitudes of Clerical and Manual Workers', *Sociological Review* 12-13.

Timperley, S.R. and Gregory, A.M. 1971. 'Some Factors Affecting the Career Choice and Career Perceptions of Sixth Form School Leavers', *Sociological Review* 19.

Titmuss, R. 1962. *Income Distribution and Social Change*, London.

Titmuss, R. 1965. 'Goals of Today's Welfare State', in Anderson and Blackburn (eds.), 1965.

Urry, J. and Wakeford, J. (eds.) 1973. *Power in Britain*, London.

Weber, M. 1968. *Economy and Society*, (in 3 vols.), New York.

Wedderburn, D. and Crompton, R. 1972. *Workers' Attitudes and Technology*, Cambridge.

Wedderburn, D. and Craig, C. 1974. 'Relative Deprivation in Work', in D. Wedderburn (ed.), *Poverty, Inequality and Class Structure*, Cambridge.

Westergaard, J. 1965. 'The Withering Away of Class: A Contemporary Myth', in Anderson and Blackburn (eds.), 1965.

Westergaard, J. 1970. 'The Rediscovery of the Cash Nexus', in R. Miliband and J. Saville (eds.), *The Socialist Register 1970*, London.

Westergaard, J. 1975. 'Radical Class Consciousness: A Comment', in Bulmer (ed.), 1975.

Westergaard, J. and Resler, H. 1975. *Class in a Capitalist Society*, London.

Wilensky, H.L. and Edwards, H. 1959. 'The Skidders: Ideological Adjustments of Downward Mobile Workers', *American Sociological Review* 24.

Willmott, P. and Young, M.D. 1960. *Family and Class in a London Suburb*, London.

Woodcock, G. 1962. *Anarchism*, London.

Worsley, P. 1964. 'The Distribution of Power in Industrial Society', in Halmos (ed.), 1964.

Young, M. and Willmott, P. 1956. 'Social Grading by Manual Workers', *British Journal of Sociology* 7.

Young, M. and Willmott, P. 1957. *Family and Kinship in East London*, London.

Zeitlin, I.M. 1968. *Ideology and the Development of Sociological Theory*, Englewood Cliffs.

Zweig, F. 1961. *The Worker in an Affluent Society*, London.

Index